PRAISE FOR *PODCASTING MARKETING STRATEGY*

'A definitive guide to everything you need to know about podcasting.'
Gemma Butler, Marketing Director, The Chartered Institute of Marketing (CIM)

'Podcasting continues to be one of the highest-impact forms of content marketing, and guides to the subject don't get more comprehensive than this.'
Kelvin Newman, Founder and Managing Director, Rough Agenda (the company behind BrightonSEO)

'A comprehensive guide to the world of podcasting. This book will help you create a podcast – but far more importantly, it will help you create a powerfully loyal audience for it.'
Rebecca Moore, Arts Marketing Association (AMA)

'This book is a really practical guide to both podcasting and podcast marketing – it covers absolutely everything you need to know. If you are already on your podcasting journey or are just starting out, this is a must-have guide.'
Tracy Hastain, Founder and Director, Wentworth Consultancy

Podcasting Marketing Strategy

A complete guide to creating, publishing and monetizing a successful podcast

Daniel Rowles
Ciaran Rogers

KoganPage

Publisher's note

Every possible effort has been made to ensure that the information contained in this book is accurate at the time of going to press, and the publishers and authors cannot accept responsibility for any errors or omissions, however caused. No responsibility for loss or damage occasioned to any person acting, or refraining from action, as a result of the material in this publication can be accepted by the editor, the publisher or any of the authors.

First published in Great Britain and the United States in 2019 by Kogan Page Limited

2nd Floor, 45 Gee Street	122 W 27th St, 10th Floor	4737/23 Ansari Road
London	New York, NY 10001	Daryaganj
EC1V 3RS	USA	New Delhi 110002
United Kingdom		India
www.koganpage.com		

© Daniel Rowles and Ciaran Rogers, 2019

The right of Daniel Rowles and Ciaran Rogers to be identified as the authors of this work has been asserted by them in accordance with the Copyright, Designs and Patents Act 1988.

ISBNs

HARDBACK	978 0 7494 9854 2
PAPERBACK	978 0 7494 8623 5
E-ISBN	978 0 7494 8624 2

British Library Cataloguing-in-Publication Data

A CIP record for this book is available from the British Library.

Library of Congress Cataloging-in-Publication Data

Names: Rowles, Daniel, author. | Rogers, Ciaran, author.
Title: Podcasting marketing strategy : a complete guide to creating, publishing and monetizing a successful podcast / Daniel Rowles, Ciaran Rogers.
Description: London ; New York : Kogan Page, [2019] | Includes bibliographical references and index.
Identifiers: LCCN 2019004540 (print) | LCCN 2019006797 (ebook) | ISBN 9780749486242 (Ebook) | ISBN 9780749498542 (hardback) | ISBN 9780749486235 (pbk.)
Subjects: LCSH: Podcasting. | Marketing.
Classification: LCC TK5105.887 (ebook) | LCC TK5105.887 .R69 2019 (print) | DDC 302.23/40688—dc23
LC record available at https://lccn.loc.gov/2019004540

Typeset by Integra Software Services, Pondicherry
Print production managed by Jellyfish
Printed and bound by CPI Group (UK) Ltd, Croydon CR0 4YY

To Susana, Teresa and Charlie: Chickocrats.

Daniel Rowles

This book is dedicated to Stella, Amelie and Izzy, for all the help and support you so freely give.

Ciaran Rogers

CONTENTS

Part Two Building your business case and plan 33

FOREWORD

The business environment is rapidly changing and the fast-paced world and level of noise in digital media are a real challenge for organizations of all types. Podcasting offers a personal and highly emotional connection to your audiences, which can often be missing via other digital channels.

At the Chartered Institute of Marketing (CIM) we see time and time again that practitioners and those studying business of any type (whether they consider themselves marketers or not) need to make closer connections with their target audiences at scale. Podcasting offers a rare combination of both intimacy and scalability. Knowledge of both the strategic impact and the tactical issues around podcasting is increasingly important, particularly as the adoption and usage of podcasting are growing rapidly.

Daniel and Ciaran have worked extensively with the CIM, helping our members and customers to navigate their way through this exciting and fast-moving environment. They form a well-respected authority on all things digital, and as such are the ideal guides for your journey into effective podcasting.

Chris Daly, Chief Executive, CIM

Part One
Podcasting in perspective

.

Stand out from the social media noise

01

Why you should be podcasting

In the early days of digital marketing, we would build websites and use on-line advertising to shout 'Buy our stuff!' at people. We then got a little wiser and started using content marketing, and embraced the idea of using con-tent to engage with our audience even when they didn't want to buy stuff. The problem, however, is that everybody has embraced content marketing, so there is an awful lot of content. This level of 'noise' continues to grow and, for example, there are around 74.4 million blog posts published each month (Wordpress, 2018), which equates to around 2.5 million blog posts being published every day. There are also around 576,000 hours of video uploaded to YouTube every day (*Business Insider*, 2018). That's over 65 years' worth of content being uploaded every day! The bottom line is that if you want somebody to consume your content, it's getting increasingly hard.

So surely podcasts are just more content and more noise? Potentially, but actually they are very different to all other forms of online content in the way in which they are consumed. The majority of people listen to podcasts not when sitting in front of their computer (although many do), but rather via their smartphone when they are on the move (Nielsen, 2018). Also, as a longer-form type of content, we engage with them for longer than we do a blog post or a short video. They also generally form part of a series, so we listen again and again. This different pattern of consumption has a huge impact on how effective podcasts can be.

In this book, we will show you how you can plan, create and distribute highly engaging and successful podcasts. We'll also show you how these podcasts can drive your objectives and how you can measure and demon-strate your success. Ultimately, you'll learn how podcasts can make you or your brand stand out above the online noise.

One of my favourite ways to demonstrate just how noisy social media has become, and the level of content being produced, is to use a fantastic website called Internet Live Stats. It shows how many social media posts and how much content have been published so far today, based on the time zone you are in, and you can see it grow in real time. You'll find it at www.internetlivestats.com

As well as podcasts being consumed differently, they can also connect to people at an emotional level and build more trust than other digital channels. People trust podcasts as a source of information more than both blogs and video (Nielsen, 2018) Why? Basically, because you are listening to a human voice/voices and it therefore feels more intimate than reading a blog.

The growth of podcasts

We'll look at podcast adoption in detail in the next chapter, but at a top level, the number of us listening to a podcast weekly has grown by 58 per cent over the past two years (Todd, 2018). What's interesting, though, is that podcasts are still an unknown to many people, with only around 30 per cent (Richter, 2018) having listened to a podcast in the last month. This leaves huge room for growth.

The barrier to entry

So, if podcast adoption is growing so rapidly and podcasts get great engagement and different media time, why is everyone still writing blog posts? There are a whole host of reasons, but one of the most important ones is that it appears harder on first inspection to record a podcast than to write a blog post. We actually don't think this is true at all.

We all have what we need to create a blog post easily to hand in most cases. If we have a word processor or text editor of some description, we can write pretty much anywhere. Podcasting, however, requires some equipment that not everyone has, such as microphones and an audio recorder (although you'll see that just a smartphone can often be enough) plus a decent audio environment for recording in (not too noisy, too much echo, etc). Once these two factors are taken care of (and we'll talk about them a lot more in this book) we actually think that recording audio is actually easier than writing, particularly if your podcast involves dialogue between two or more participants. We've spent our entire lives learning to talk and discuss, so this comes more naturally to many people than the apparently more structured process of writing.

We've already said that only about a third of us regularly listen to podcasts, and this level of adoption is often cited as a reason not to use them. However, bear in mind that these adoption figures are higher than for many social channels like Twitter and LinkedIn (Smith and Anderson, 2018). And podcasts are growing more quickly, whereas the use of channels like Facebook is declining in many markets (Smith and Anderson, 2018; Sterling, 2018).

Podcast passion

In our minds, though, the most important thing about podcasts is the level of engagement and advocacy they can drive. If people care enough to listen to what you have to say every week for 30 minutes, they are quite likely to have a fairly strong opinion about you and what you say. I (Daniel) think that a quote I heard from a fellow podcaster and former colleague of mine, Kelvin Newman, who runs the world's largest SEO conference BrightonSEO, sums it up brilliantly:

People who like podcasts, really really like podcasts.

We'll hear more from Kelvin later, but he's really onto something here. The average podcast listener listens to around seven shows per week and 80 per cent are listening to all or most of the entire show (Winn, 2018).

In my experience as a podcaster, the level of advocacy, that is people who are willing to share your content and say nice things about you, is at an incredibly higher level than with other forms of content and social channels.

Content or channel

We would normally refer to things like Facebook, YouTube or Instagram as digital 'channels', which contain different forms of content such as audio, video text and images. So, are podcasts content or a channel? Well, podcasts are a specific format of audio that is distributed as a series in a specific way (via iTunes or Spotify, for example). We think therefore it's fair to consider podcasts as a channel in their own right, but many people would disagree and argue that they're just a specific audio format. Essentially it doesn't really matter, but we just need to be clear that when we compare different digital 'channels', it's not always a completely like-for-like comparison, so we need to be considered in our approach.

The podcast opportunity

Hopefully what you can see from this first brief introductory channel is that podcasting offers a fantastic opportunity to cut through the level of noise that exists online, build an audience, drive engagement and essentially drive your desired outcome. What we haven't even touched on yet, though, is the limitless creative opportunities that podcasting actually offers. Whether you're doing a live interview-style podcast recorded directly onto your smartphone, or a high-production, multiple-section podcast with extensive post-production, the only limit is your imagination. This book will help nurture and inspire your ideas, and then help you turn those ideas into a success.

PODCAST INSIGHTS   **Podcast inspiration**
Bethan Jinkinson, Executive Editor, BBC Ideas

I first got hooked on podcasts when someone recommended *Serial* series one to me. It blew my mind – it was a fascinating true-life tale, cleverly told and hugely addictive. After that, my podcast journey took me in all sorts of directions. From comedian Romesh Ranganathan's *Hip-hop Saved My Life* to the sublime *This American Life* (listen to the episode called Abdi and the Golden Ticket – it's life-changing). My most recent addiction has been to Radio 4's *The Ratline*, a brilliant WW2 tale of twists and turns, which also asks profound questions about what it means to be human, and what being on the right side of history really means.

In my current role as executive editor of BBC Ideas (short films for curious minds – bbc.com/ideas, check it out) I get a lot of inspiration from podcasts; they expose me to all sorts of ideas and corners of history.

I always learn something from Malcolm Gladwell's *Revisionist History* (probably one of the best podcasters on the planet).

Podcasts have also exposed me to creative thinking in terms of my role as a leader. My favourite of that genre is Bruce Daisley's *Eat Sleep Work Repeat*, a fascinating podcast on workplace culture. Podcasts have also taught me more than I thought I wanted to know about economics (the BBC's *50 Things That Made the Modern Economy*) and food (the delightful *Table Manners* with Jessie Ware and her mum).

The best advice I can give an aspiring podcaster is to listen to tons by other people. What do you like about them? What grates on you? What made you click on one podcast and not another? Who has recommended podcasts to you, and what would you recommend? Develop your critical thinking and take inspiration from the ever-growing podcast world around you.

Something else to bear in mind is sound quality. I was a former digital editor at BBC World Service, the BBC's international radio network with a huge podcast footprint (including the seriously brilliant *Global News* podcast). Coming from a radio background you become really aware of the well-mixed, well-balanced and well-edited content. It really stands out.

Finally, remember that for the listener, podcasting is an intimate medium. You make an active choice to listen. You can stop at any time, skip to another podcast. It's not like radio, which kind of washes over you and you're never quite sure what's coming next. So make every second count, keep the narrative driving forward, and keep surprising your listener. You want to give them insights and inspiration that they'll be talking about on social media, or down the pub. In my experience, word of mouth is a huge driver for discovery, so make sure your podcast is being talked about online and in real life.

The Digital Marketing Podcast and online resources

Throughout this book we'll refer to our own podcast, the *Digital Marketing Podcast*. With over 200 episodes under our belt, millions of listens and a constant presence in the iTunes top 20 business podcasts, we've learned a lot along the way. We'll try to help you learn from our mistakes and successes and share data and insight you won't find anywhere else.

Accompanying this book you'll find a host of online resources, including a list of all the tools and websites mentioned in the book: www.targetinternet.com/podcastbook

References and further reading

Number of blog posts

Wordpress (2018) A live look at activity across Wordpress.com [online] https://wordpress.com/activity/

Amount of YouTube content

Tran, K (2017) Viewers find objectionable content on YouTube Kids, *Business Insider* [online] https://www.businessinsider.com/viewers-find-objectionable-content-on-youtube-kids-2017-11?utm_source=feedly&utm_medium=referral

Podcast consumption and trust

Nielsen (2018) A marketer's guide to podcasting [online] https://www.nielsen.com/us/en/insights/reports/2018/nielsen-podcast-insights-q1-2018.html

Podcast adoption

Richter, F (2018) The state of podcasting, *Statista* [online] https://www.statista.com/chart/14306/podcast-adoption/

Todd, L (2018) Your summer podcast guide: why 2018 is the year of the 'podcast boom', *BBC* [online] https://www.bbc.co.uk/news/entertainment-arts-44714155

Social media usage

Smith, A and Anderson, M (2018) Social media use in 2018, Pew Research Centre [online] http://www.pewinternet.org/2018/03/01/social-media-use-in-2018/

Facebook decline

Sterling, G (2018) Pew survey finds marked decline in Facebook user engagement since March, *Marketing Land* [online] https://marketingland.com/pew-survey-finds-marked-decline-in-facebook-user-engagement-since-march-247469

Kelvin Newman

Newman, K (2017) Why podcasting is the missing piece in your inbound strategy & how to excel in audio content [online] https://www.slideshare.net/kelvinnewman/ why-podcasting-is-the-missing-piece-in-your-inbound-strategy-how-to-excel-in- audio-content-theinbounder

How many podcasts

Winn, R (2018) 2018 Podcast stats & facts (new research from Dec 2018), *Podcast Insights* [online] https://www.podcastinsights.com/podcast-statistics/

Podcast adoption

Growth and expansion of podcasting as a popular medium

We're pretty sure that if you are reading this book that you are already convinced of the potential that podcasting holds. However, you may not be fully aware of the scale of opportunity or you may need to persuade others of the great opportunity on offer.

We'll focus on driving business objectives using podcasts in a later chapter, but it's important that the growth we outline here is seen in the context of what you want to achieve. My personal objectives for podcasting are numerous. The key one is to essentially drive sales for my business, but there are also huge elements of brand building, growing an audience and creating advocacy (a lot more on all of these later). You may be building a podcast to share opinions and change people's minds, to tell a story you think everyone should know, or to make yourself famous. Whatever the objective, it's worth understanding the opportunity.

Global adoption of podcasts

On average, 34 per cent of people have listened to a podcast in the last month (YouGov 2018), but as you can see in Figure 2.1, adoption varies widely by country.

High smartphone penetration together with very high levels of social media usage and social sharing in Asian countries like South Korea and Taiwan give some of the highest levels of podcast usage at 58 per cent and 55 per cent respectively. In the United States, traditionally where some of the world's most popular podcasts have originated, 33 per cent say they have accessed a podcast in the last month.

Figure 2.1   Percentage of surveyed users that have accessed a podcast
in the last month

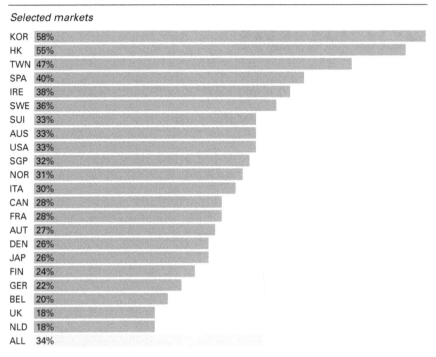

Selected markets

KOR	58%
HK	55%
TWN	47%
SPA	40%
IRE	38%
SWE	36%
SUI	33%
AUS	33%
USA	33%
SGP	32%
NOR	31%
ITA	30%
CAN	28%
FRA	28%
AUT	27%
DEN	26%
JAP	26%
FIN	24%
GER	22%
BEL	20%
UK	18%
NLD	18%
ALL	34%

Based on a YouGov survey of 74,000 online consumers

Surprisingly, podcasts seem to be accessed least in North European countries such as Finland (24 per cent), Germany (22 per cent), the UK and the
Netherlands (both at 18 per cent). Bear in mind these figures, particularly
the UK data, may be skewed downward. This is because of platforms like
the BBC iPlayer offering podcasts in a format where people don't realize
they are listening to a podcast.

Demographics of podcast listeners

As you can see in Figure 2.2, the 18–34-year-old age group is the most likely
to listen to podcasts, with nearly half those sampled saying they listen at
least monthly.

Types of content

The most popular podcasts topics are News and Politics, and Business,
Science and Media, both with 14 per cent of online users listening to this

Figure 2.2   Podcast listeners by age

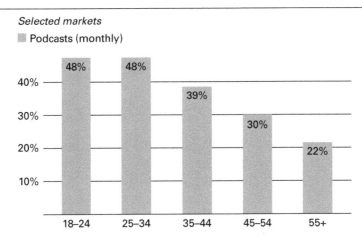

Selected markets
▨ Podcasts (monthly)

Based on a YouGov survey of 74,000 online consumers

type of podcast. Lifestyle topics come in next with 13 per cent, on subjects such as fashion, music, food and the arts. Drama series come in next at 10 per cent, and finally Sport at 8 per cent.

Demographics

Many surveys have found that the majority of podcast listeners are male in many cases; for example, in a recent study, Salesforce found the gender split was 56 per cent male and 44 per cent female (Young, 2017). However, this gender split varies by industry and topic, for example with marketing and online drama podcasts skewing towards a female audience, at 52 and 65 per cent respectively (Joyce, 2018).

Unreachables

According to research by Acast, a particular audience that podcasts can reach well, but are extremely hard to reach elsewhere, are referred to as the 'Unreachables' (Hebblethwaite, 2018):

> Choosy, on-demand media connoisseurs who know when they are being sold to – and are more likely to seek ways to avoid it.

Podcast listeners match this category very well in many cases, as they are more likely to use ad blockers (31 per cent), but they are also likely to pay for premium services (84 per cent). Podcast listeners are also willing to act on the ads they hear, with 76 per cent saying that they have followed up on an ad or sponsored message they heard on a podcast. Thirty-seven per cent have looked for more information on a product, 24 per cent have visited the brand's website and 18 per cent have shared that information online (Hebblethwaite, 2018).

High income

Another interesting and important fact about podcast listeners is that on average, they have 18 per cent higher household incomes than the average online users that don't listen to podcasts (Winn, 2018).

Passionate, affluent and young

We're not suggesting listening to podcasts will make you wealthy or younger, but the podcast audience is generally highly engaged and skews toward a young and/or high-income group. It is also an audience that subscribes, and is passionate about the podcast they give their listening time to.

New ways of listening

New ways of listening are also encouraging more people to listen to podcasts. The addition of podcasts to the widely adopted music streaming service Spotify has opened them up to a whole new audience, as well as giving existing podcast listeners another way to listen.

The growing use of 'Smart Speakers' that include artificial intelligence personal assistants, like the Amazon Echo or Google Home, allows people to search for and play podcasts via their speakers. Existing audio streaming speakers systems like Sonos now have Apple's Siri built into them and also allow for voice search and the playback of podcasts.

The number of ways of finding and playing podcasts will no doubt continue to grow, but no technology will make anybody listen to something of poor quality, so let's go on to explore why people actually listen to podcasts.

PODCAST INSIGHTS   A viewpoint on podcasts

Gemma Butler, Marketing Director, The Chartered Institute of Marketing

In a world where everything around you is moving at warp speed and you feel like you haven't got any time left for yourself, podcasts allow you to stay on the move from place to place whilst still taking the time to listen and learn. They go where you go, whether that be commuting to and from work, running on the treadmill at the gym or sat at home on the sofa: they can fit seamlessly into your life. Podcasts are a way to consume content that is not only easy and engaging, but is flexible to individuals: you choose what you want to listen to and when.

The fast-paced world of marketing has seen the role of the marketer change significantly and the need to keep up to date is all the more important. For marketers, podcasts offer a way of learning about the new tools and technologies that are thrust upon us on a daily basis. More than ever, marketers need to ensure that they stay informed and stand out in order to develop in their careers; however, this is easier said than done when your workload is at maximum capacity. CIM has worked in close collaboration with Target Internet on their digital benchmarking assessment tool, which produced a detailed view of the digital marketing capabilities across the UK. The results of the benchmark report were echoed in the research carried out during the development of the CIM Digital Diploma, raising the need for individuals and organizations to bridge the digital skills gap via ongoing learning.

Podcasts, like audiobooks, give you the freedom to shut out all the noise in a world of constant demands on your time and attention. It's a one-on-one relationship and sometimes it's good to switch off and just listen.

References and further reading

Podcast adoption

Newman, N (2018) Podcasts and new audio strategies? [online] http://www.digitalnewsreport.org/survey/2018/podcasts-and-new-audio-strategies/

YouGov (2018) Digital news report [online] http://www.digitalnewsreport.org/

Podcast gender

Joyce, G (2018) Podcast audiences: why are women such big fans of true crime podcasts? *Brandwatch* [online] https://www.brandwatch.com/blog/react-podcast-audiences/

Young, H (2017) 20 stats about the 2017 podcast consumer, *Salesforce* [online] https://www.salesforce.com/blog/2017/04/20-stats-about-the-2017-podcast-consumer.html

Unreachables

Hebblethwaite, C (2018) 23% of UK population listened to a podcast in the last month, *Marketing Tech News* [online] https://www.marketingtechnews.net/news/2018/mar/29/23-uk-population-listened-podcast-last-month/

Income

Nielsen (2018) Nielsen podcast insights: a marketer's guide to podcasting [online] https://www.nielsen.com/content/dam/corporate/us/en/reports-downloads/2018-reports/marketers-guide-to-podcasting-q3-2018.pdf

Winn, R (2018) 2018 Podcast stats & facts (new research from Dec 2018), *Podcast Insights* [online] https://www.podcastinsights.com/podcast-statistics/

Understanding how people really listen to and absorb audio content   03

To create a successful podcast you really need to get under the skin of your audience and understand how, where, why and when they are listening. There are some podcast stats that can get us the how, where and when part (and we'll share and discuss these), but the most important part is the Why.

If we take our *Digital Marketing Podcast* as an example, we can see why the Why is so important. Digital marketing is an extremely fast-paced industry that changes constantly, so there is a demand for ongoing education on the topic. Also, many traditional marketers want to cross-train into digital marketing, again creating a demand for educational content. So we can see there is a demand for the topic, but that still isn't the Why. The Why is why do they want to improve their skills and educate themselves? And the answer is to either be better at their job and have a more successful career (including making more money), or if they are self-employed, to improve the performance of their business (and again make more money). With this in mind we can understand the type of content we need to produce, but also the tone that we should use. Our answer to the Why is to focus on practical, hands-on advice that will quickly improve our audience's knowledge and give them skills to make demonstrable improvements in their work. If we make them look good at work, they'll keep listening and hopefully become advocates.

What, where and when

We know from surveying the approximate 8,000 regular listeners of the *Digital Marketing Podcast*, that at least 80 per cent of them listen while they are travelling, and the reason most often given was to make their commute more productive and entertaining. Forty-four per cent of us have now played audio from our smartphones in our cars, up from just 6 per cent in 2018 (Edison Research, 2018) because of how much easier it now is to connect our phones to our car audio wirelessly. Sixty-nine per cent of us use our smartphone rather than our computer to listen to podcasts and we listen in a range of places, including whilst travelling, at the gym, at home and in the office. Although research has shown that around 49 per cent of us listen to podcasts at home most often (Edison Research, 2018), that doesn't mean that these people aren't also listening when travelling; it's just where they listen the most (and this can be potentially misleading; they just listen more there as they spend more time there than they do travelling).

Understanding the Why: building personas

A great technique for planning all forms of content and marketing activity, and one that we have found works particularly well for podcasts, is to split your audience into its core groups and build personas to represent each of these groups. Personas are made-up individuals that represent a core group of your audience, and they have demographics and characteristics that allow you to consider what your audience cares about. So for example, if we create a persona who we'll name Susana, we can look at our podcast content, format or tone and ask ourselves, 'Does this work for Susana?' However, just because personas aren't real people, it doesn't mean their characteristics should be completely fabricated. They need to be based on insights into your target audience, otherwise you can create a persona that bears no resemblance to reality and will drive your podcasting efforts in totally the wrong direction.

Example persona for the *Digital Marketing Podcast*

Name: Susana

Age: 39

Location: London

Job: Start-up Company Director

Goals:

Wants to drive her business forward and generate more revenue.

Wants to feel comfortable and confident in discussing digital marketing-related topics.

Wants new ideas and insights to come up with new business ideas.

Challenges:

Very short of time as works long hours, has family commitments (see below), has a small team to support her and commutes.

Her background is in business rather than marketing and she has limited knowledge of the technical aspects of digital marketing.

Watering holes:

Heavy Twitter user following digital marketing and start-up influencers.

Engages in regular conversations on LinkedIn with other start-up founders.

Listens to podcasts like *Masters of Scale*.

She reads online magazines like *Fast Company* and *Wired*.

Reads commuter newspapers like the *Metro* and *Evening Standard*.

Personal background:

Family-oriented with two children.

Keen on fitness (but has limited time) so doesn't always prioritize gym over work.

So, what can we learn from this persona? Well, first of all we know that our content needs to be educational and practical to apply. It must be time-efficient to consume so episodes can't be too long. It also can't be too technical and should not rely on the audience having huge budgets to apply the techniques taught.

We also know she is already familiar with podcasts, but the time limitations she faces, the fact she commutes and likes to go to the gym but doesn't always see it as an efficient use of time, fit really well with further podcast adoption. When creating any promotion for the podcast, as well as within the podcast itself, we need to highlight how it's an efficient way to learn and can be done at the same time as doing something else.

Every time we plan a new episode we can ask ourselves, 'Does this work for Susana'?

Working with multiple personas

It's very unlikely that your audience will consist of just one persona. It's much more likely that there will be several and that they may have some goals and challenges in common, but some may differ. The key is creating content that works for most of your personas, most of the time. You might find that the occasional episode doesn't work for a particular persona, but an audience will generally forgive you the occasional episode that isn't quite right for them. However, if you bring an audience in with relevant content, then produce episode after episode that isn't right for them, you're going to lose them.

What do you do when your personas have very different needs and very different challenges, and the same content won't ever work for both of them? You really then need to consider if it's possible to cater for both audiences with a single podcast, or if you need to do a separate podcast series for each audience. Or maybe you need to reconsider whether you are really going to target both audiences.

Using a content calendar can help you plan your content, but also help you keep an eye on what personas you are providing content for, and any that you keep missing. We'll explore this more in Chapter 10.

Speed of content

It's interesting to note that 19 per cent of podcast listeners say that they use the functionality in the app or device they listen on to speed up the playback rate of podcasts (Edison Research, 2018). This is an important insight in that it tells us that people want to get to the important and relevant content quickly, without having to listen to lots of content they may feel is filler, or less relevant; in many cases they will speed up advertising sections if they don't add value. In our experience, if you spend too much time 'telling people what you are going to tell them', they quickly get irritated and impatient. It also means that pre-roll advertising is probably not delivering much value to advertisers and very often irritates listeners.

Bringing it all together

To get your podcast right you need to understand who your target audience is, what they want and what is motivating them. We'll explore the idea of the user journey and what it means to this process in a later chapter, but we really need to align five key things to get our podcast right. We need clarity on who our audience is, what their objective is, where they are in the journey to achieving that objective, what *our* objectives from the podcast are, and finally, what our 'brand positioning' is, that is, our tone and how we present ourselves. We'll explore these topics in more detail in the coming chapters.

Reference

Device, location and playback speed

Edison Research (2018) The infinite dial 2018 [online] https://www.edisonresearch.com/infinite-dial-2018/

Building genuine 04 personal engagement through podcasting

One of the greatest advantages of podcasting is the ability to deliver an intimate experience at scale. The fact that you are listening to a human voice, or voices, and every human voice is unique, means we can deliver personality quickly and easily with our content. It's not that you can't deliver personality with text, but it is harder and takes longer. Also, although you can deliver personality via video, the fact that podcasts are audio only means that our mind is focused on interpreting the voice we hear; combined with our audience's imaginations, we can take people on journeys that would need serious special effects budgets to achieve in video! Emma Rodero, a communications professor at the Pompeu Fabra University in Barcelona, was interviewed in the *Atlantic* on the viral success of some non-fiction podcasts and succinctly explained this point:

> Audio is one of the most intimate forms of media… you are constantly building your own images of the story in your mind and you're creating your own production.

Masters of Scale podcast

By far one of my (Daniel) favourite podcasts is the *Masters of Scale* show. It covers the world of fast-growing businesses and is hosted by Reid Hoffman, the founder of LinkedIn. Reid's big personality comes across very effectively due to his engaging tone and industry expertise, but what's fascinating is how they use clever production to bring each of their interviews and stories to life. I advise every budding podcaster I meet to listen to at least a few episodes, so they can understand how a combination of great content, an original format and great production can help produce a chart-topping podcast.

The podcast uses a combination of the hosts speaking directly to the listener to build a narrative, interviews and sound bites from their guest on the show, and clever production techniques using effects and additional voices, to make and reinforce points throughout the show. Every episode is well concluded and, very importantly, all content is aimed at a very clearly defined audience, and provides value to that audience.

Podcast personality and value proposition

When creating podcast content we need to be clear on what personality we are delivering, and this will come from both what we say and how we say it. We also need to consider what our value proposition is, that is, what value are we providing and how would we summarize that? Our general advice has been that the format of your show will have a huge impact on how you go about delivering the right personality and tone, and how you deliver your value proposition. You need to make active decisions about how you want the podcast to come across and what the core value proposition is.

Value proposition

Our value proposition basically sums up what the core value and benefit of our podcast will be. It's not a commercial objective, but what value it offers the audience. So, as a company that sells digital marketing e-learning, our podcast positioning is not 'The world's best digital marketing e-learning', it's actually 'Practical and hands-on digital marketing advice'. That is what our audience wants, and it gives us a standard against which to test all of our content. If it doesn't deliver on that value proposition, it's not the right content.

Personality and tone

We'll explore the most common formats in a moment, but let's consider tone and the use of language. We have all developed our own personalities over the duration of our lifetimes, and you can use these as part of delivering the overall personality of your podcast. However, don't forget that 'podcast you' doesn't have to be the real you. Let's explain with a couple of examples.

First, let's consider how we use social media in a professional context. My (Daniel) Instagram profile (@targetinternet) is not the real me. It's just me in a professional context. And although there are plenty of lighthearted pictures and it's not particularly serious at all, you won't find pictures of my kids, my wife, my family life or my weekend activities. It is a consciously crafted version of what I want to project, and it therefore curates the parts of my life I want to communicate. If I want to project the things that are more personal to me, I'll connect with you via Facebook. It's not that my Instagram account isn't genuine, but it is a considered and consciously crafted personality with a defined tone. A podcast should be the same. There is certainly a place for podcasts that are 100 per cent unfiltered and genuine, but this again should be a considered decision.

Another example of this conscious effort to construct a personality for your podcast, tied in with the hosts' own personalities, is our own *Digital Marketing Podcast*. We use a conversational format, and we'll outline what this means in a moment. However, when you use this format, the dynamic between the two people speaking is really important. Our general approach is that Ciaran, my co-host and co-author of this book, basically plays dumb on a topic, and asks me questions to try to extract the right practical information for our audience. He may well know more about the topic than I do, but he uses this knowledge to extract the right answers from me that will be useful to our target audience. This technique is often used in the interview format as well, as a good interviewer will have prepared extensively, and even maybe know what answers to expect in advance of asking them. Ciaran is so effective at using this technique that when people meet him, and realize his huge level of knowledge and experience, they are often quite blown away. The risk is that this could come across as quite 'constructed' and fake. However, this risk is neutralized by what else we do in the podcast. If you listen to a few episodes, you'll notice that there is a fair bit of banter between the two of us, and this comes from our many years of working together and experience of recording hundreds of episodes together. We consciously don't edit this banter out (unless it gets really silly!), as this again helps to build the personality of the show. We each have a role to play, and we play it within the bounds of the podcast's personality and tone.

Analysing tone using artificial intelligence

A tool we've been playing around with recently is the Personality Insights tool from IBM's artificial intelligence Watson. Watson, amongst other things, is fantastic at analysing text, whether that is a series of tweets or, most importantly, a transcript from a podcast. You can analyse a few well-known Twitter accounts to get a feel for how it works, and you can then upload your own text to see how your tone is coming across, and whether it aligns with your planned podcast personality. Bear in mind this version of the tool is just analysing your text, rather than your tone of voice, so the way you are speaking can change things completely. However, it does give some fantastic insights and is very interesting, so it's well worth a try: https://personality-insights-demo.ng.bluemix.net/

Podcast format

The format of your podcast is one of the most important decisions you will make, as it has a huge impact on how well you connect and engage with your audience. It also has a big impact on how much work your podcast will need, so choose carefully. We've outlined the most common formats and their potential advantages and pitfalls. We've also included a few examples for you to listen to and learn from. The core formats are:

- interviews;
- conversational;
- information;
- solocasts;
- non-fiction storytelling;
- fiction.

Interviews

A classic in the podcasting world, interview shows generally feature a consistent host (or hosts) and a new guest each episode. They give the audience a chance to learn from the expertise and experience of people in a particular niche.

A great example is the *Tim Ferriss Show*, one of my favourite podcasts, and certainly the one I've been listening to for the longest. In Tim's own words, 'Each episode, I deconstruct world-class performers from eclectic areas (investing, sports, business, art, etc) to extract the tactics, tools, and routines you can use. This includes favourite books, morning routines, exercise habits, time-management tricks, and much more.' The quality of the guests is off the charts, having featured people like Arnold Schwarzenegger and Jamie Foxx, but what's most interesting to me is the format. They are fairly unedited interviews and they are also generally long. Very long. Many episodes are over two hours, and although this is fairly unusual, it clearly works for his audience.

Advantages:

If the interview flows, these types of shows don't often need a lot of editing.

It's a fairly simple format in order to produce regular content.

Pitfalls:

Finding and organizing the right quality of guests can be challenging. No end of people want to be interviewed, but getting people that interview well and have something interesting to say is not always easy.

People that 'um' and 'err' a lot can be very difficult to listen to on a podcast, so screening guests first can be important.

Conversational

Listening to a conversational podcast feels like overhearing a chat between two friends. Usually these types of shows have multiple hosts, and episodes could feature discussions on a focused topic (like digital marketing in the *Digital Marketing Podcast*) or a broader range of things based around a core topic (like the *Random Show*, part of the Tim Ferriss podcast).

These types of shows are easy to listen to (it's why many radio shows have two presenters), they are easy to record, and tend to be between half an hour and an hour long. Listeners will tune in because they like the content as well as the hosts' personalities. Because of the conversational format, they'll feel more connected to the hosts than to those reporting a story in a news show for example.

Advantages:

Easy to record once a dynamic has been created.

Easy to listen to and a popular format.

Pitfalls:

You need to get the two co-hosts together on a regular basis, which might
not always be easy, depending on geography and other commitments.

Interview vs conversational

As the two most common formats, which is best? There is no right answer
to this question, but there are a couple of points to consider. It's a lot easier
to get the conversational format working and consistent, as by definition, in
every episode of an interview format a major variable changes, and that's
one of the speakers. One of the reasons some interview-based podcasts
tend to be in a longer format, is that it can sometimes take a little time to
get into a groove with a new interviewee.

We interchange between the two formats, using mostly conversations
and then intermingling them with interviews. However, we can see really
clearly from our stats that if we do a series of interviews we start to lose
listeners, as we are not appealing to the core base that likes the
conversational format.

There is no doubt that a good interview-based podcast can be insightful
and a real pleasure to listen to; they are just hard to get working really well.

Information

These can often be a higher-production variation on the interview podcast,
but potentially with multiple hosts, interviewees and cuts between different
sections. Think of them as the documentary series of the podcast world.
The aim is to communicate a topic on a theme each episode. My favourite
example, mention earlier, is the *Masters of Scale* podcast, hosted by Reid
Hoffman, the founder of LinkedIn. It educates its target audience on les-
sons learned in the start-up world about how to scale businesses quickly
and effectively. The level of production work is incredible and it's consistently my favourite podcast.

Advantages:

Highly engaging format.

Opportunities to use original formats and production techniques to communicate your points.

Pitfalls:

Needs much more planning.

Needs more time and resourcing for production.

Solocasts

Solocasts feature monologues on a topic that's important to the creator. The episodes tend to be based on the creator's own experience and could be anything from comedy to advice-based content. Generally, our advice has been that a dialogue is easier to listen to than a monologue, but it really depends on the skills of the speaker. If you think of how we listen to audiobooks, these are really the same format.

Someone whose voice and opinions I (Daniel) could listen to all day long is Seth Godin, and his podcast *Akimbo*, whilst not strictly a solocast, as he does feature guests from time to time, is mostly just his voice. And it's fantastic. So, what makes it work, when it's a format that often fails? First of all, Seth is a fantastic writer, with a library of best-selling books already having sold millions of copies. His podcasts are clearly very well planned and written. He is also incredibly passionate about what he's speaking about and has given each topic a lot of thought. This is not an easy format to do well, but when it works it's fantastic and builds a hugely connected relationship with your audience.

Advantages:

No co-host or interviewees, so fewer logistical and planning issues.

Can be a simple format to record and edit.

Can build great intimacy with your audience.

Pitfalls:

Needs high levels of planning.

Needs even higher levels of passion and knowledge than elsewhere.

No one to riff off and bounce ideas around with (although this can be addressed).

Non-fiction storytelling

This is the single format that has grown podcasting more than any other in recent years. Real-life crime investigation dramas like *Serial* have grown phenomenally and have opened podcasts to a whole new audience. The art of storytelling is not an easy one, but when it works, it can transport an audience to a different place. They don't need to be on the epic scale of *Serial*, but could simply be a current affairs show that communicates a story using narrative.

You could tell one story across a season or keep it short and have a new story for each episode. Shows in this format usually involve fairly high levels of production, using audio clips from different interviews and narration to inform the audience of what they need to know to get a complete understanding of the story.

Advantages:

Opportunity to use narrative to create a highly engaged user.

Storytelling can transport an audience like no other style of audio.

Pitfalls:

High production and planning levels required.

Not always easy to get it right and create compelling stories.

Fiction

There is already a large industry around fiction audio books, where a story is narrated, and this can be a similar format, but generally for shorter stories or by serializing a longer story.

You can also really go wild in terms of creativity and production, and this format is nothing new at all. We've had radio plays for many years, and when successful they can transport the listener to another world or time.

Advantages:

Narrative-based formats can grow audiences quickly when they work.

Huge creative opportunities.

Not a particularly widely used format so there is lots of scope for growth.

Pitfalls:

Needs extensive writing and production.

Not a particularly widely used format so many people aren't looking to podcasts for this type of content.

Format crossover

There are no rules that say you must pick one format and only use that format. Although consistency can help you build an audience (as they know what to expect and they like your show they will come back and expect more of the same), you can still experiment with formats. Look at your podcasts stats (more in a later chapter) to understand what content is popular and what isn't. Most of all, actually ask your audience. We really can't state this point strongly enough. Actually speaking to your audience and getting feedback will stop you double guessing yourself, but will also make your audience feel more engaged and appreciated.

PODCAST INSIGHTS   The podcast process

Kelvin Newman, Founder and Managing Director, Rough Agenda, the owners of BrightonSEO, the world's largest SEO conference

There's no question that podcasts have had a huge impact on both my own personal development and the businesses I've promoted with them. The intimate and personal relationship a podcaster can build with an audience is unlike any other form of content marketing. Over time the trust and respect a podcaster can build is huge. The benefits to me, though, weren't just promotional but also in terms of confidence. The time spent preparing for a podcast had an amazing role in clarifying my thoughts on a subject and really helped me think about the best way to explain some tricky and complex ideas. I thought I knew a lot about how to explain a topic until I tried to pull together a podcast on that area. When I worked to explain something using audio it really helped me take the time to make sure I was explaining it clearly and concisely. It made me a better public speaker and a better person to work with.

Producing a podcast forces you to go beyond your comfort zone, and for me that meant approaching and interviewing some of my absolute professional heroes. After having friendly conversations producing podcasts with the kind of people who've had *New York Times* bestsellers and TED talks with more than a million views, and realizing they are just normal people too, it really changed my perspective on business and the opportunities for me in the space.

I've never been daunted by editing audio. The tutorials available online for any software platform are incredible, plus if you listen back to the first few episodes of some of your favourite podcasts you'll realize that everyone sounds a little rough around the edges initially. There's not a single podcast out there where the sound and quality of production hasn't improved over time.

Further reading

Podcast engagement

Wen, T (2015) Inside the podcast brain: why do audio stories captivate? *The Atlantic* [online] https://www.theatlantic.com/entertainment/archive/2015/04/podcast-brain-why-do-audio-stories-captivate/389925/

Part Two
Building your business case and plan

How to use podcasts to drive business results

05

One of the first things to consider when planning any podcast is why are we doing it and what is our desired end outcome. In this chapter we'll explore the different reasons for creating a podcast and start to consider how a podcast can drive our desired outcomes. We'll also start to look at how we can measure the success of our podcasts.

To make things easy, we can pretty much put any business into one of three boxes:

1 An e-commerce business that wants to drive an online sale. Their online objective is the same as their business objective.

2 A lead-generation business that wants somebody to fill in a form or pick up the phone and call. Their online objective is a form/call but the business objective is an actual sale that may happen later.

3 A brand-based business that wants some sort of online interaction, such as listening to a podcast, but then wants something to happen elsewhere, like somebody walking into a store to buy something or voting a particular way in an election.

If we define these online objectives as our Primary objectives, we can start to look at how somebody listening to a podcast can help drive these Primary objectives.

Podcasting for the sheer joy of it

Podcast objectives may fall into the desire to deliver something creative and build an audience to react to that content. You could consider this as just podcasting for the sheer joy of podcasting, and as people who thoroughly enjoy creating podcast content and seeing what reaction it gets, we fully understand why you might do this.

Although there may not be a 'business objective' in these cases, there are still things we can measure to judge success against our initial objectives and we'll start to explore some of those here (we'll look at measurement in more detail in Part Three of the book).

So how does someone listening to our podcast help drive these business objectives? Let's consider a few scenarios:

Direct action: I listen to a podcast, hear about a product or service and I go to a website or pick up the phone and buy straight away.

Indirect action: I listen to a podcast, hear about something I can do online/offline, like download a whitepaper, sign up for a newsletter, or attend an event, and then through further communication and interactions I end up buying your product or service.

Brand impact: I listen to your podcast and because I enjoy it and/or find it useful, my perception of your brand improves. Then at some later time I select your product or service because I recognize and trust your brand.

In all of these scenarios the podcast has a central role to play in driving our desired outcomes, but measuring its impact has some challenges which we'll come to in a moment.

Driving your objective

You can go about this in a number of ways, but what you can't do is make the key focus of your podcast selling your product, service, political party, charity or anything else. The podcast is there to provide value, it's not a sales channel. The question is, how directly can and should you drive your desired outcome?

Let's use the *Digital Marketing Podcast* as an example. Our business objectives are to sign people up to our digital marketing e-learning, either individually or as a team, or to book a face-to-face training course. So we have both e-commerce and lead-generation-based online objectives. But we also have a number of smaller objectives, like getting people to sign up for a newsletter, sign up for a free membership, carry out a skills benchmark or download some premium content.

How much should we promote each of these objectives? Well, we know that if we basically fill the podcast with promotions for our services, it will soon irritate people and we'll lose all our listeners. So, what do we do in reality? The podcast starts with a sponsorship message: 'Welcome to the *Digital Marketing Podcast*, brought to you by TargetInternet.com'. We then may mention in the podcast what we've been working on and encourage people to sign up for a free offer, such as a downloadable guide. The real objective is to get them to the website and collect some data so we know who they are. Then, at the end of the podcast, there is a more direct sales message, but these are changed and rotated with different offers, so that they are always fresh and don't sound too pushy.

This has been a very effective strategy for us, both for driving direct sales, but also for building trust and brand awareness over the long term. Most interesting to us is the amount of large business-to-business orders we take from global brands, where the podcast was a contributing factor but we only find this out after or during the sale. We'll very often meet up after we have signed the business and people will saying something along the lines of how funny it is meeting face to face as they recognize our voices. This brings us back to the level of connection we can build using podcasts.

The challenges of podcasts

Although we love podcasts and have proven how they can contribute to our business objectives and drive revenue, there are some distinct measurement challenges. Fundamentally you will be able to track how many people listen to your podcast, but initially you won't know anything about them. The only way to find anything out is to drive them to an action, such as signing up for an email or filling in a survey. Driving somebody to your website or app is always desirable, so you can at least expose them to the things you have to offer. This is where things like 'show notes', the landing pages for our podcasts, really come into their own. From here we can drive whatever action we desire, but there has to be enough value on the website or app. Without that value, our audience won't make the effort to go from listening to doing a search or typing in a website address. We have a whole chapter dedicated to landing pages and related topics like Search Engine Optimization coming up (see Chapter 12).

Beyond the last click

Analytics (explored later) allows us to see activity on our websites and apps, and where that traffic has come from. It also allows us to track our desired outcomes, at least to some extent. What we need to be clear on from the outset, however, are the limitations of analytics and what it can't tell us.

Generally, many web analytics reports take a 'last click' approach. This means we look at some form of activity, such as a download, and see where the traffic came from that directly preceded the download. What this doesn't tell us are all the steps before that last step, particularly if they were something like listening to podcasts.

Just because I came to your website from a search engine and then downloaded something, doesn't mean the search engine was solely responsible for the download. I may have visited your website 10 times before, from multiple sources over an extended period of time, and the first step may have been initiated by listening to a podcast. This is what we really need to understand. Thankfully, by using some relatively new features in tools such as Google Analytics, this has become a lot easier.

Analytics also can't measure when our outcomes happen offline, such as when our sales come in over the phone or at a showroom. Does this mean that tracking in analytics is a waste of time? Not at all, it just means we need to be clear on what we want to achieve online and that this should be as close as possible to our actual desired business outcomes. I define these online goals – which may not be our actual business objective but are as close as we can measure online – as 'primaries'.

Primaries are the key things that we can monitor online that are as close as possible to our business objectives. If you sell online with a credit card facility, then your 'primary' will be a sale. However, if you are looking for leads it may be forms submitted or calls made to a web-advertised telephone number. It could also be the registration for an event or the download of a very relevant piece of content. These are not our absolute business objectives in many cases, but the closest we can come online to achieving these.

Effective measurement can help differentiate exactly what role each piece of marketing, including podcasts, played through to the completion of the user journey.

The common challenge for measuring the success of any podcasting activity, whether online or offline, is that our final conversion – be that a sale or completion of some other task – may happen via a channel that is disconnected from our marketing activities. For example, it could be a sale on someone else's website, an order taken over the telephone or a booking made via a third-party supplier. What we aim to do in this section is show you an effective technique for bridging these gaps between our end objective and our podcasting efforts.

Traditional brand metrics

Generally we would take some sort of sample survey of our audience and see what their attitudes were before and after exposure to some form of marketing, such as listening to a podcast. This survey would ask a range of questions, and there are lots of different approaches, but fundamentally we are looking to answer these questions:

Are you aware of the brand?

Do you like the brand?

Do you intend to buy the brand?

If you have purchased, do you intend to do it again?

Essentially we are assuming that if we can get more people to answer positively to each of these questions, we are likely to get more sales. We can therefore say that if someone who listens to a podcast is more likely to say yes to these questions, then a podcast listen is a measure that we can consider a proxy for success.

However, what we can now do is take all of the data we have from web analytics and podcast measurement tools and combine it with traditional surveying techniques to create a feedback process that allows us to continuously improve our marketing activity.

Understand the value of every marketing activity

We should be able to calculate the value of every bit of our marketing activity and look at how it is contributing to the bottom line. The reports and analytics we can now get may not give us a 100 per cent perfect approach, but it is a lot closer to reality than how we've been measuring things in many industries up until now (if we have been doing any measurement at all!). Those elements we called 'brand building' in the traditional sense basically meant that we didn't really know how much they contributed to the bottom line, but we were pretty sure they did.

Later we'll suggest a practical combination of techniques that map out all the steps of the user journey and see how they contribute to our end objectives. That way, every step is understood and nothing needs to be labelled as 'brand building' but can actually be measured effectively.

For perfection we need a mind-reading device

A perfect approach to marketing is impossible unless we can read minds. This is because even using surveying techniques, when you ask someone questions about why they did something they often have no idea, or recall things incorrectly. For example, if you ask someone why they buy a particular detergent, they probably have no idea. We can put this down to branding, but it still doesn't give us any detailed information. As long as there are humans involved, there will always be some level of uncertainty involved in measurement.

Digital shot itself in the foot

One of digital's greatest problems has been self-inflicted. In the heady days when digital marketing first started, we happily claimed that everything could be measured and that traditional offline marketing was dead. This was a little arrogant, to say the least. You can measure everything if it ALL happens online. So if you only market online and you make a sale online with a credit card, then you can measure most things. What it doesn't take into account is a scenario where the only reason your customer searched and found you on Google in the first place was because they listened to a podcast in their car the night before. While we still have these kinds of problems with digital, we can nonetheless now measure a lot more than just pure online transactions.

TV has culture, podcasting doesn't... yet

If you spend a few million pounds on a TV campaign, you're probably quite likely to spend some money on finding out what it did for you. And in fact, many agencies that work on TV will factor in some budget for calculating the effectiveness of your campaign into your overall costs. To be fair, if you're spending £2 million on a campaign, £10,000 doesn't seem like much to spend on calculating value. However, if you are spending £500 on producing a podcast, you're not going to spend the same again on finding out if you got ROI, because even if you did, you won't have done once you pay to work it out!

So we need to develop a culture of starting out with the concept that all digital activity will be measured – and that we can do this relatively easily and in a cost-effective way.

Filling the gaps

The most important thing we are trying to do is to fill in some gaps. Does positive engagement with our podcast actually lead to sales? We assume so but we don't actually know. Does more people listening to our podcast mean we sell more? We assume so, but not necessarily. We will try to fill these gaps by demonstrating how measurement – and asking questions – can provide the answers.

Abandoning volume

One of the key problems with looking at volume-based metrics is that they don't give you an indication of what success actually looks like. You may feel that getting 10,000 listeners is a great success. However, if your nearest competitor has 500,000 listeners, it's suddenly a very different story.

Volume is prevalent in social media measurement but also in other digital channels as well. We look at things such as how many emails we have sent, or the number of page impressions or unique visitors to our websites. These are not so much a measurement of success or failure but rather indicating factors that can lead to our actual desired outcomes.

Benchmarked measures

To get away from purely focusing on volume-based measurement in podcasting we can do a number of things, and in the measurement chapter we look at an approach that ties in web analytics. However, even without getting into analytics we can do some simple things to give us much more practical information. We need to try to benchmark our measurement, and there are a couple of ratio-based podcast measures that are easy to use (but are fairly rarely used).

Share of voice is a great ratio for understanding where you sit in relation to your competitors, and for judging the success and reaction to your podcasting efforts. You will need a social media listening tool to calculate this, and for many channels there are free tools that will do the job.

You start by measuring the total level of conversation around the topic area you are concerned with. For example, a recent client of ours looked at the conversation around skin care. The easiest way to do this is to look at one channel at a time. So, for example, how many tweets there are around the topic of skin care within a particular geographic region (you can do this using the Twitter advanced search).

You find this out by deciding on a set of keywords and phrases that you want to monitor, and then looking at the level of conversation on these phrases. You then repeat this process, but just identify the tweets that were specifically about (or mentioning) your podcast, brand or product/service. You will then have two numbers: one for total conversations on the topic and the other for conversations about your product. Divide the number of conversations about your product by the total number of conversations on the topic, and you have your 'share of voice' percentage. This may be very low, but you can continue your podcasting efforts and then take the measurement on a regular basis (normally monthly is sufficient). Progress made in increasing this percentage gives you a more useful guide than just looking at the number of tweets or likes. The other great thing about this measure is that you can calculate it for your competitors. You then have a benchmarked measure that can give you an indication of how effective your efforts are, and how that compares to your competitors.

Audience engagement is another percentage that you can easily measure and benchmark against your competitors. We tend to look at it on a platform-by-platform basis so that we know our audience engagement for Twitter, Facebook, LinkedIn, etc and can make efforts to improve this. Again, we normally measure this on a monthly basis.

You start by looking at the size of your overall audience on a particular social platform, such as Facebook or Twitter, and then consider how much of that audience is actually engaging with you. So, for example, if you have 10,000 likes on Facebook, and when you post a podcast you get 1,000 likes on that piece of content from your likes, then your audience engagement is 10 per cent.

We need to define what we mean by engagement. On a platform like Facebook there are multiple ways to engage, as you can like, share and comment on a post. We would count any of these activities as engagement. With Twitter we consider a reply or a re-tweet to be engagement, and so on. Technically speaking, if the same user were to carry out multiple engagement activities on the same platform on the same piece of content, we should probably not count these more than once. In practice, however, it doesn't actually matter as long as you are comparing like for like. As well as taking this measure for your own social platforms, you can very easily analyse your competitors as well.

Benchmarking and business results

Although benchmarked measures don't relate directly to business results, they are far more connected to helping us achieve our objectives than just looking at volume-based metrics alone. We could again see these as a proxy for success. Realistically, if you are targeting the right audience your share of voice is growing and your audience engagement is increasing – you are in a strong position. There is still a gap between this and actual sales, but we are getting closer.

The next stage is to connect these social media measures to our web analytics and business objectives, which we look at in the next section.

Measurement comes in many forms

We need to combine a number of different measurement techniques in order to really understand the impact of each piece of our marketing activity and particularly with podcasting. This includes using basic web analytics, podcast analytics, marketing attribution tools and, finally, chopping up some data in spreadsheets or dashboarding tools like Google Data Studio. It is not as painful as it sounds, but the reality is that it is neither easy nor something that most podcasters know how to do. This is one of the fundamental issues surrounding calculating ROI that we need to be clear on. It needs to be planned from the outset and is a process we need to build, repeat and improve.

PODCAST INSIGHTS   **Delivering business results through a conversational podcast**

Laura Poulton, Head of Marketing, Affinity, Aon Risk Solutions UK

I started listening to the *Digital Marketing Podcast* a few years ago, and it's safe to say it is one of my 'go to' marketing and digital marketing podcasts. Daniel and Ciaran have a way of delivering engaging and relatable content into bite-sized chunks, and it's easy enough to pick and choose what's relevant for my role and industry. I've used many of the tools with my teams, and have used some podcasts (eg the one about cognitive bias) as workshop resources.

In Summer 2018 I reached out to Target Internet for consultative support with our digital strategy and working with Daniel has been a great experience to date. Once again I'm getting practical advice and tools to use, but this time tailored to my specific requirements.

For more on measurement and analytics, head over to Chapter 22 and Chapter 24.

Understanding the role of podcasts in the user journey

06

We'll now look at the role of podcasts in the user journey. The user journey is the route a target audience takes to get to where we would like them to be (if, for example, we wanted them to buy a product, their journey would be the route they would take before making this decision). Understanding where the audience is on their user journey is important when determining how podcasts can add the most value and help to accomplish our goal. When used at the beginning or middle of the journey, they can assist in drawing an audience in, building a relationship with them and encouraging them along the path to the end point we hope they will eventually reach. This chapter will focus on how podcasts can be fitted into the user journey and the best way they can be used to engage our target audience.

The role of podcasting in multichannel marketing

With all marketing it's very difficult to pinpoint just one single interaction with a customer that prompts them to favour a particular product or brand. Multichannel marketing means that there tends to be a number of factors which combine to encourage customers to make the choices that they do along their user journey. Podcasting forms an integral part of multi-channel marketing strategy, as it can be used to influence customers over a period of time.

Digital marketing means that we are in a better position than ever before to understand and measure the buying process, and as marketers we have a number of tools at our disposal to help us to do this. We often have access to enormous amounts of data which can help us to understand the decisions that our buyers make. What is often less clear, however, is how our online and offline marketing strategies interact with each other. For example, how many times might our customers have revisited the different online and offline content, and in what order? It's unlikely to be a linear journey and we are not privy to all of it. Mobile can sometimes help us to bridge this gap but it's not straightforward and does present its challenges. That said, we do have a better understanding than ever before, and with a little forethought we can get a clearer picture of how the different channels are working together.

Two different types of user journey

So how might we fill in these gaps and gain a better understanding of how our different channels are interacting? We'll now look at two different examples showing user journeys right up to the decision to purchase. The first shows a business-to-business (B2B) user journey and the second a real-life business-to-consumer (B2C) journey.

A B2B user journey

A customer who is responsible for their business's website is looking for a new hosting company. The website has been down recently, which the customer feels embarrassed about, and they are eager not to repeat the experience. The customer's main concern is therefore reliability, as they would like to reduce the chance of the website going offline again, but they will also weigh up the following factors before making their buying decision:

- Performance – they need the website to be as fast as possible.
- Flexibility – they might be interested in developing the website in the near future.

The customer needs to gather as many facts as possible before making their decision, and throughout their user journey the steps they take will include, but will not be limited to:

- Subscribing to a technology podcast to hear about other people's views and experiences.

- Performing several online searches for suppliers.

- Searching for online reviews of these suppliers.

- Subscribing to these suppliers' communications.

- Using their social network to gather opinions, for example, Twitter or LinkedIn.

- Undertaking diagnostics to understand the type of hosting they need.

- Visiting websites to learn about the technology behind hosting, and signing up to these websites' communications to help educate themselves further.

- Discussing with colleagues and partners at events unrelated to the website and, through these discussions, being recommended other suppliers that they haven't yet come across. They will make a note of these suppliers on their phone.

The following are important things to consider in light of this decision-making process:

- The customer's decision is being led by the need to minimize the risk of the website going offline in the future.

- The customer feels a need to educate themselves on the topic (which is often the case in B2B purchasing decisions).

- The journey is done almost entirely online, apart from the face-to-face interactions.

- The technology podcast drives the supplier search as that is where the customer first hears about many of the suppliers.

- The customer spends much of their user journey offline (either on a train with poor signal or on a plane) so therefore reads a lot of the information without internet access.

So what are the key takeaways from this scenario when thinking about our podcast activity?

- Risk mitigation, trust and education are important themes and these would need to be at the centre of our value proposition.

- As a potential supplier we would need to go further than just telling the customer that our solution is the best; in order to gain their trust, the customer needs us to educate them on what we can supply and why it is needed.

- We would need an effective and active social media approach as the customer relied heavily on this channel to help them make their decision.
- The customer needed content that they could consume on the go, which would work on all of their devices without needing constant internet access.

A B2C user journey

We'll now look at a real B2C example from one of our own experiences. I have amassed a number of airline loyalty points, and want to find out what I can do with them. I need information about how the process works, as well as ideas for places to visit. I am very much looking forward to investigating different destinations so, for me, the process is as much about enjoyment as it is about being able to form any kind of practical plan.

The steps I will take throughout this process will include, but will not be limited to:

- Trying to find out how many points I have by logging into my online account.
- Gaining an understanding of how the process works.
- Seeing how far I can go with my points and getting a list of possible destinations for where my points could take me, despite not having a particular place in mind.
- Discovering when flights are available.
- Considering my options in terms of destinations, types of holiday, and suitability for different types of travel (family, couple, etc).
- Gaining inspiration and insight by signing up to a travel podcast.
- Thinking about how to use my points in the most cost-effective way, bearing in mind airport taxes and other charges.

Much of my research was done on a mobile device, which is unsurprising given that one of my main drivers was to have fun and 90 per cent of smartphone users use their phones whilst on the go to progress towards a long-term objective (Think with Google, 2018).

Sadly, I did not find this process easy, and in fact, with the airline I had chosen, it turned out to be almost impossible to have the enjoyable experience I had hoped for. Below are some of the reasons why:

- I was redirected from the main site to a mobile site which was difficult to use.
- There was not an easy way to return to the main website.
- The main website did not have the capability to work across devices.
- The search options didn't suit my needs as I didn't have a particular destination in mind.
- Browsing availability was cumbersome and time-consuming as I had to scroll through multiple pages of dates.
- I was hoping for further information or links to other websites to guide me on potential destinations, which the site didn't include.
- I signed up to the travel podcast for inspiration and insight, but it was just focused on selling.
- I needed information on options when travelling with my family (important as I wanted to be sure we could all sit together on the plane, etc).

The airline went wrong because they hadn't considered people's different user journeys and the various ways in which they could engage their audience to build their trust. The technology didn't fail them – they did have an app – but they fell down because they mapped the process to their booking system rather than thinking about customers' different motivations and needs. Had I found the process easier, I might have made a booking, but even if I hadn't booked there and then, they would have increased my brand loyalty, making it more likely that I would return in the future or recommend them to others. A good podcast would have been their ideal opportunity to engage me and get me on board.

The podcast I signed up to was all about selling, but this should not be the main driver when designing podcast content. Remember that I wanted to use the tools to *be inspired* and *plan*. A good podcast could have helped me to do this, and I might have gone through the whole process apart from the actual booking, returning to book a few weeks later once I had considered all my options. It is so important to recognize the potential value in preliminary visits to websites even if they don't result in a sale. In Chapter 24 we will look at this in more detail, and specifically something called 'multichannel funnels' in Google Analytics, which could help with this scenario.

Using podcasts as content marketing

The idea behind content marketing is to provide your audience with helpful, interesting content suited to their user journey. It is not to directly promote a product or brand, but rather to provide added value that will engage the customer and help build their trust. Thinking about the B2B user journey example above, the podcast would have been much more effective had it focused on providing useful information for the user about web technologies rather than selling. Table 6.1 gives a few more examples of how different types of companies might effectively focus their podcast content for good content marketing.

Enhancing brand and value proposition through podcast content

Providing digital content or services in this way enhances our brand's value proposition. Furthermore, the more creative we are with how we use digital technology to deliver the content, the more opportunity we have to interact with our audience and, through this interaction, gather data and a more comprehensive understanding of who is actually listening to our podcast. This, in turn, helps us to build a closer relationship and bolsters trust in our brand. Table 6.2 gives some examples of how the podcast themes outlined in Table 6.1 could be implemented in an interactive way.

These ideas are all very simple, but with a bit of development, they all have the potential to significantly increase a brand's value proposition. It's important to note the same principle can be applied to any organization, regardless of their product or service offering. Purchasing decisions can generally be divided into high involvement (as in the B2B example above, where the

Table 6.1 Ideas for content marketing themes

Type of company	Focus of podcast content
SEO agency	Digital marketing advice
White-water rafting (aimed at teams)	Team building and human resources
Alcoholic drink brand	Cocktail making and recipes
Detergent	Family money-saving tips
Sportswear	Training and fitness tips
Business service	Thought leadership articles

Table 6.2   Content marketing themes and interactivity ideas

Focus of podcast	Interactive idea
Digital marketing advice	Campaign reporting tool
Human resources	Interactive HR guide with scenario planning
Cocktail making and recipes	Interactive portable recipe book
Family money-saving tips	Coupons and location-based savings
Training tips	Training objective progress tracker
Thought leadership articles	Interactive audio/video tutorials

customer felt the need to carry out a lot of research before making their decision) and low involvement (an example would be buying a chocolate bar; you'd be unlikely to go online and research your options before deciding which one to get!). However, regardless of whether a purchasing decision is high or low involvement, well-positioned, digitally delivered content marketing can significantly strengthen a brand's value proposition.

Illustrating the steps within the user journey

All online user journeys consist of a number of steps or stages, generally progressing from unfamiliarity with a product, topic or brand all the way to an intention to purchase and (you hope!) loyalty to the product or brand once the purchase has been made. A number of different models are used to illustrate this process. The best place to start is a traditional sales funnel model. We will also look at the See, Think, Do, Care framework.

A user journey using the traditional sales funnel

Figure 6.1, showing a traditional sales funnel, illustrates how someone moves along their user journey, starting with simply browsing and having a vague notion of their requirements, progressing to having an active interest, then on to purchase and post-purchase loyalty. As the funnel shows, this is not a linear process, and differing amounts of time can be spent in each stage. For example, the active interest phase can vary in length depending on the target audience and the service or product that is being offered. It also shows that the loyalty stage is by no means the end of the process –

Figure 6.1 The traditional sales funnel

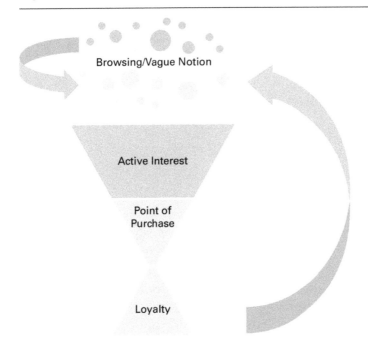

Browsing/Vague Notion

Active Interest

Point of
Purchase

Loyalty

a customer may well still be interested in content intended for the browsing stage once they have been through the funnel and are in the loyalty stage.

Organizations need to understand their target audience's intentions, needs and motivations in order to provide well-targeted content and interactions to encourage them on to the next stage. We'll shortly go on to consider exactly how this content, and specifically podcasts, can be mapped to the different stages in the funnel.

A user journey using the See, Think, Do, Care framework

The See, Think, Do, Care framework is the brainchild of Avinash Kaushik, author, expert in analytics and Digital Marketing Evangelist for Google. The framework is described in his blog, *Occam's Razor* which you can read about here: http://www.kaushik.net/avinash/. The framework is a straightforward, adaptable and powerful model for planning content which, like the funnel model, demonstrates the need to map different forms of content to each step of a user journey.

Fitting podcasts into the user journey to enhance our value proposition

We will now use both of these models to show how podcast content can be mapped against each stage, using two contrasting organizations. TargetInternet. com is a B2B company which delivers online digital marketing courses and Tesco.com is a global online retailer which sells groceries and other products.

Table 6.3 sets out the different stages of the traditional sales funnel model and the See, Think, Do, Care framework, and maps these against examples of content that could be used in order to target a particular audience. As the table shows, at the See (Browse) stage, the suggested content is quite general in nature. As progress is made throughout the journey, the content becomes more specifically related to the products sold by each organization. For example, at the Think (Active Interest) stage, the Tesco content is related to healthy ideas for children's lunchboxes. At the Do (Point of Purchase) stage the content relates to each organization's main product offering. Once customers get to the Care (Loyalty) stage, their needs are more general again, and the content offered is the same as at the See (Browse) stage.

So in order to get the foundations of a good podcast content plan, we need to carefully map out the needs and motivations of our various target audiences,

Figure 6.2   Avinash Kaushik's See, Think, Do, Care framework

Table 6.3 User journey models and content mapping

Stage	TargetInternet.com	Tesco.com
See (Browse)	7 top Facebook tips for social success	25 things to do with your children on a rainy day
Think (Active Interest)	Complete guide to bridging the digital marketing skills gap	20 healthy ideas for children's lunch boxes
Do (Point of Purchase)	Online digital marketing courses	Online grocery shopping
Care (Loyalty)	7 top Facebook tips for social success	25 things to do with your children on a rainy day

and the different user journeys they might take. Our content plan can then be aligned to our business goals and measured for success to form the beginnings of our digital strategy.

Making the best use of our digital channels

In order to form a robust digital strategy, we will also need to understand how to make the best use of different digital channels. To help illustrate this, we will now have a brief look at an online tool from Google, 'The customer journey to online purchase' (see Figure 6.3). This is one of many really useful free tools offered by Google and we will use it to help understand which digital tools are best suited to which stage of the user journey.

This tool is based on a model that divides the user journey into four main stages: awareness, consideration, intent and decision. It then maps different channels against these stages to determine how effective each channel is at each stage of the process. As you can see, in B2B marketing, social media is most likely to be used at the beginning or middle of the process, with email and paid search being more suited to the later stages before a purchase is made. This helps us to understand which channels we should be delivering our podcast content through at each stage, bearing in mind that podcasts are generally most effective in the earlier stages. It also shows us that social media is a powerful tool for building awareness, suggesting that this would be a great way to deliver our podcast content in order to engage our target audience and start to build a relationship with them. This example is, of course, specific to B2B selling and it does not necessarily apply to other markets; however, it helps us to start to think about things in a certain way.

Figure 6.3 Google's 'the customer journey to online purchase' in action for the B2B category in the UK

Explore how marketing channels for Large ▾
businesses in the Business & Industrial ▾ industry
in The U.K. ▾ influence the purchase decision.

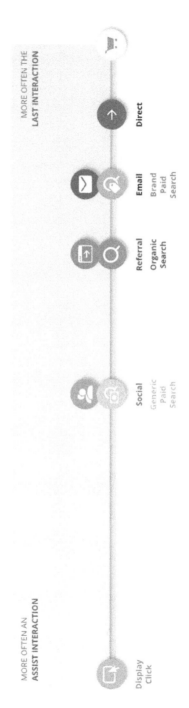

MORE OFTEN AN
ASSIST INTERACTION

MORE OFTEN THE
LAST INTERACTION

Display
Click

Social
Generic
Paid
Search

Referral
Organic
Search

Email
Brand
Paid
Search

Direct

Channels to the left tend to play an early and assisting role in the typical sale,
while channels to the right are more likely to be the last interaction before a
purchase.

(Google and the Google logo are registered trademarks of Google Inc, used with permission.)

Understanding the terminology: goals and conversions

We will use the terms 'goal' and 'conversion' throughout this book so it is useful to define them here.

A *goal* is something we are hoping our target audience will do. This would normally be an online activity and could be buying something, listening to a podcast or filling in a form. A *conversion* happens when the goal has been completed.

When these terms are thought of in relation to our podcasting and other digital marketing, we can begin to appreciate their importance in terms of our objectives and overall digital strategy.

Reference

Mobile usage

Think with Google (2018) Mobile [online] https://www.thinkwithgoogle.com/advertising-channels/mobile-marketing/

An introduction to podcast marketing 07

There are a number of ways people can listen to your podcast, and generally you are relying on people knowing what a podcast is and how they can listen to them. Even then, they need to find your podcast within their chosen listening environment (iTunes, Spotify, etc). So what we need to do is make sure we are discoverable when people actively look, but also push ourselves out there for people who aren't actively looking.

In this chapter we'll introduce the need and concepts behind podcast marketing. In Part Three of this book we'll explore a range of techniques to practically deliver this marketing, including social media channels, influencer and advocate outreach, display advertising and email marketing. We'll talk about Search Engine Optimization in Chapter 12, when also we talk about landing pages, and about naming and describing your podcast to maximize discoverability.

> We talked previously about levels of podcast adoption, but what we didn't discuss is those people who don't listen, maybe don't know what a podcast is and certainly don't know how they might listen. For the 40 per cent of people (Newman, 2018) who don't know anything about podcasts what can we do? With the *Digital Marketing Podcast* we took a very simple approach, and it grew our podcast audience by 5 per cent. We simply created a blog that explained how you can listen to a podcast and then walked people through the process step by step. We then used a range of the marketing options below to promote the post across a range of digital channels. You can see the blog here: https://www.targetinternet.com/how-to-listen-to-the-digital-marketing-podcast/

Part Three explores a range of the digital tools and channels at your disposal in order to deliver your podcast to your potential audience.

The guidance, tips and tools highlighted here have all been drawn from our own experience of planning and implementing digital campaigns for a wide range of organizations around the globe, from global film franchises through to chemicals that go into paint to make it whiter. The surprising thing is that most of these organizations have exactly the same problems and challenges when trying to build a podcast audience. However, they may need to approach these challenges in slightly different ways, using different channels to achieve their desired outcomes.

In the previous chapter we discussed the user journey; podcast marketing is about selecting the most appropriate techniques to interface with that user journey in order to help create the value that we discussed. That basically means getting your podcast in front of the right people, at the right time on the right digital channels.

We will also explore the idea of not making too many assumptions and making sure we always operate a 'test and learn' approach. A great example that we've learned through our own business demonstrates this well. The *Digital Marketing Podcast* we publish is aimed at marketers and business people generally, and as such it is a business-to-business (B2B) podcast. As we all probably already know, generally speaking, Facebook is not a place for B2B. However, as an experiment we launched a Facebook page for the podcast to try to test if this assumption was correct. It took little resource, as we basically used the platform to post links through to the content we were already creating and to generate some feedback on this content. We had little expectation but thought it a low-cost test worth a try.

The results were surprising, to say the least. We now have nearly 25,000 people who have liked the page, engaged with our content and driven traffic back to our website. This engagement drive signals back to Google, which in turn pushes us up the search rankings. I know of at least one very major project we have won because of the awareness this created and it gives us a place for two-way dialogue with our audience.

Pragmatic curiosity

This guidance in Part Three is a practical hands-on guide to using digital channels in the real world in a time-efficient way. However, it is also essential that we don't ignore potential options because of untested assumptions and that we don't become afraid of the new.

Digital marketing is generally moving at an incredible pace, and this is not going to slow down. It is very easy, and often sensible, to be suspicious of the never-ending flow of new channels and to adopt an 'I'll use it when it's been proven' approach. We do need to commit, however, to trying things out, albeit in a pragmatic and sensible fashion.

Latest tools and techniques

Let's face it, by the time you read this there will be lots of new stuff that has happened between the time of writing and the book going to print. For that reason, we will be filtering and highlighting on the website that accompanies this book. We would also love your feedback and we're happy to publicize your podcast efforts and experiences: http://www.targetinternet.com/podcastbook

---

Reference

Podcasts and new audio strategies?

Newman, N (2018) Podcasts and new audio strategies? *Reuters Institute* [online] http://www.digitalnewsreport.org/survey/2018/podcasts-and-new-audio-strategies/

What differentiates a great podcast?

If we could give you a formula here for what would make your podcast a 100 per cent guaranteed success we would. But we're afraid we can't, and unfortunately neither can anyone else. What we can do, however, is share our experience, a few opinions and some case studies from podcast experts.

Clarity on value proposition

Let's start with my own experience and some hard-learned truths. For the *Digital Marketing Podcast*, there are two key things that make it work. The first is having absolute clarity on our value proposition: 'Hands-on, Practical Digital Marketing Advice'. It allows us to focus in on exactly what type of content we should be creating, and even more importantly what we shouldn't. When we are running a planning session, and as we build our bullet points of what we are going to discuss, very often we'll get half-way through and just dump the idea if it doesn't feel quite right. The mantra of 'If there is any doubt, there is no doubt' should be applied. If some content or an interviewee doesn't really feel like it's the right quality, don't put it in, especially if you are just doing it to make sure you get an episode out on time. Consistency is incredibly important, but we know from experience that it's better to not put out a poor episode and be a little late than to publish when you are not ready. Our analytics tell us that when we put out a dubious episode (it's normally an interview, where the interviewee didn't live up to what we were hoping for, but because of scheduling we didn't have an alternative episode to put out), our numbers drop next time as we lose part of our audience and they don't come back. Stick to your value proposition and focus on quality.

The pitfalls of interviews

If you are proactively seeking out the right people to interview, doing your background research and interviewing people who are used to being interviewed and speaking in public, you are on the right track. What often happens, however, is that as your podcast grows in popularity, people (and their agents) start approaching you to be interviewed. This doesn't mean that these people won't give you a great interview, but in my experience the outcomes can be mixed. More often than not these people have a business agenda (which isn't always a bad thing if they approach it without being too pushy) but they also have very different levels of interview and speaking skills. The interviewer should have sufficient skills to draw the very best from anyone they interview, but unfortunately, these skills can only go so far.

Hosts' dynamic

The other key element that makes the *Digital Marketing Podcast* work is the dynamic between us (Daniel and Ciaran), the co-authors of this book. This dynamic has been developed over a long period and many hours and conscious effort have gone into it. We have worked together for many years and recorded hundreds of episodes together and have learned when to interrupt, when to hang back and when to disagree with each other. We have even made a bit of a fine art of taking the mickey out of one another. We know each other's poor recording habits (I (Daniel) say 'absolutely' way too much when I agree with something, and Ciaran leans back from the mic). We have developed hand signals we use when recording to say when we want to interrupt or when we need to change tack, and most importantly we know we can disagree with one another without causing any offence.

All of this shared experience, and both professional respect and friendship, comes across in the podcast and people warm to it. They actively tell us so and it works for us.

Content is king

Yep, content is king, but like we said at the very beginning of this book, there is a whole lot of content out there, and therefore a lot of kings. The key here is quality and differentiation. We should go back to our user journey and make sure we're adding value for our audience and doing so in a way that is interesting, useful and entertaining. Even the driest of topics can be brought to life with narrative, so make sure you're clear on how you will communicate your content. A podcast like *Masters of Scale*, which we have mentioned a couple of times in this book, manages to align all of the key elements. It aligns an understanding of the target audience, high-quality content, a clear value proposition, great personality and fantastic production. It's not an easy feat to achieve, but it is the reason it's such a popular podcast.

PODCAST INSIGHTS   The *Ten Words* podcast

Jeremy Waite, host of the *Ten Words* podcast, author and award-winning public speaker

> *The* Ten Words *podcast is a very original format and it's fascinating to understand the thinking and process that goes on behind this highly successful podcast.*

My podcast is called *Ten Words*, so it's a very specific remit. It's usually the story of one person who has changed their life, other people's lives or an industry with a 10-word statement, so my podcast is simply looking at what those 10 words are and then going behind the scenes to look at what did they say, how did they say it and why did they say it? But the process is pretty simple. I use the same process as a lot of political strategists and in fact I got this from David Axelrod who worked on the Obama campaign. He said, there are only three things to consider when you craft a message in a piece of content: Is it important? Is it relevant? Is it true? It's those three things, and the intersection of them. If you imagine them as a Venn diagram, that's my podcast: what's important, what's relevant and what's true. So each weekly episode is going to be on something that has just happened, like the launch of the Alexander McQueen documentary might be when I do the Alexander McQueen episode. I've got to be excited about the topic as well. Once I get excited, I'm just going to scribble down loads of ideas. You can see these in the show notes of all my podcasts. Then I put it on Post-it notes and I go and attack a wall with a thousand different ideas.

Then I organize the Post-it notes into a structure, which is the same way that I do all of my presentations, which again, you'll see in the show notes, but it's based on Nancy Duarte's model. So then I draw the presentation, I draw the podcast, and then all of those clips are segmented on my computer, turned into audio files and dropped into BossJock, where after about 10 or 15 hours of prep by this point, I then just record the whole thing in one take with no editing, and as soon as I finish it's uploaded to Libsyn and the whole thing goes live.

What is digital branding and how does business development fit in? 09

Let's start by saying what digital branding isn't. It isn't about logos or visual identity and it certainly isn't about celebrity endorsements and big sports team sponsorships. What digital branding is really about is the sum of our online experiences. These online experiences may be influenced and impacted by logos and sponsorship, but we need to understand branding to be something much more than visual identity. Podcasts can form a very strong part of our overall digital branding.

Branding has fundamentally changed because of digital media. Digital has led to two-way communications between brands and consumers; social media means that we can now talk directly with the brands that we use every day. In fact, most communications via digital media don't even involve the brand anymore and are now directly between consumers. We only need to look at review websites such as TripAdvisor to realize that what consumers are saying about us is more important than what we are saying about ourselves.

A traditional view of branding

When I say that branding isn't about visual identity or logos, many people will be shocked. I'm not saying that these things are not important, but what I am saying is that they are an increasingly small part of a much more complicated picture. Your logo and the visual aspects of your website design will certainly impact on a consumer's perceptions of your organization, and they mustn't be overlooked, but the reality is that we now experience things in our connected world in a much more complicated way than previously.

The number of different online touchpoints (points at which we are interacting with a topic, product or organization either directly via something such as a podcast, website or app, or indirectly via a search engine results page or a social media discussion) we make before making a purchase are increasing. We are seeking more sources of information and are assigning trust differently. Gone are the days when marketing consisted of putting your product into the hand of a celebrity in a shiny 30-second TV commercial and thinking your efforts were complete.

This shift to dialogue rather than broadcast means that the traditional approach to branding is no longer sufficient. We need to understand how podcasts, search, social media and mobile are impacting our target audience's perceptions of us and their likelihood of buying our products. We also need to do this in a measurable way.

It's all digital

Although this book is about podcasting, it is not only digital channels that create your brand; it is every experience that your target audience has of you, from your call centre employees' tone of voice through to the type of paper you print your business cards on. The fundamental shift, however, is that all of these things are tied together by an online experience.

Brand awareness as an excuse

Brand awareness is a phrase that is often used as an excuse to justify digital activity, such as podcasts, that haven't had clear objectives set against them.

Let's take another example. Many organizations have Facebook pages. Yet most organizations have no idea as to why they have a Facebook page.

Business to business

When we talk about brands and consumers it is easy to assume we are talking about a business-to-consumer (B2C) situation. In fact, all the principles we are discussing apply equally in a business-to-business (B2B) environment as well. As the potential customer in a B2B scenario, we are still an individual going through a decision-making process. Although the buying cycle may be different and the decision-making process motivated by different factors, we can still map out and understand how digital branding is having an impact.

In reality, the process of mapping the impact and value of our podcasts in B2B is even more apparent because the majority of B2B purchases are actually made offline and we need to understand what roles podcasting and our digital branding are playing in making that sale.

What digital branding really means

A traditional view of branding says that a brand is: 'Name, term, design, symbol, or any other feature that identifies one seller's good or service as distinct from those of other sellers' (American Marketing Association Dictionary, 2018). In fact, the word brand is derived from the Old Norse word *brandr*, meaning 'to burn', and was used in reference to marking cattle by burning the owner's brand onto them.

This idea of branding has been developed over the years to factor in a far more extensive set of considerations. As well as this idea of visual identity we may also consider the thoughts, feelings, perceptions, images, experiences, beliefs, attitudes and so on that are associated with a brand. This set of considerations builds up our *brand image*, and we may also talk about our experience of a brand as our *brand experience*. The best way of thinking about it, in my opinion, is that brand is the *personality* of something.

How digital has changed branding

If you could only get a feel for someone's personality by them telling you things about themselves, we may end up with a very shallow understanding of them. We may also have difficulty believing in the personality that has been constructed – and we may start to question the motivations behind what they are telling us about themselves. That is exactly the situation of commercial branding that uses broadcast channels such as TV. A personality is sculpted and then we are told what the personality is. We don't get to discuss, engage with and really understand the true personality.

Digital media now means, however, that the conversation is no longer one way. I can challenge, ask questions and develop a truer picture of the brand. I can see through a sculpted brand and start to see it for what it truly is. This can be a scary thing for many traditional brands. It can also be a huge opportunity. This is why our podcasts should always be accompanied by ways in which our audience can interact with us. We go into this in detail in the Podcast Marketing section in Chapter 23.

Brand democracy

I (Daniel) was originally switched on to the idea of brand democracy by a good friend of mine and renowned inspirational speaker, Jonathan MacDonald. Brand democracy is the idea that your brand isn't what you say it is, but rather the sum of what everyone else says it is. This has huge implications for not only how we manage our brands, but also on how we need to change the very nature of our organizations. Podcasts can really help do this.

You can read Jonathan's original, and often challenging, thinking at the website: http://www.jonathanmacdonald.com.

Global soapbox

If brand is essentially the personality of something, digital media gives us the ability and opportunity to understand the *true* personality of something. We can then use that understanding to help guide us in our decision-making processes.

This is a great opportunity from a customer point of view. For example, it means that instead of being put on hold for an hour when phoning a call centre and having little choice but to tolerate it, I can now go straight to one of many social media channels and make my frustrations very clear and very visible. I now have a global soapbox with access to all of the other potential customers out there, and I can impact a global organization's brand in a way that was not possible before (or, at least, was incredibly difficult). That highly visible complaint then becomes part of other people's brand perception (fairly or not) and suddenly the years of building a brand can be tumbled very quickly. This is a very much changed environment for businesses to operate in – if they ignore this change then it can lead to problems.

This ability to engage with and research into a brand can also be looked at from an even simpler point of view. Perhaps I am researching buying a car or a B2B service. I can now do a lot of research and inform my decision before I speak to the car dealership or service vendor. When I do make this final step I am far more informed and have developed a fairly in-depth perception of the brand.

Where podcasts fit in

If we have considered what our value proposition is and what personality our brand will convey, we know our target audience and their journey, and understand the role of digital branding, hopefully we can see that podcasts are an ideal channel for bringing all of these things together. Podcasts allow us to build and strengthen our brands, which means they can help drive all of our business objectives.

PODCAST INSIGHTS   How they can be used to support ongoing learning

Rebecca Moore, Programme Producer, Arts Marketing Association

At the Arts Marketing Association (AMA), our core belief is that learning is essential to meaningful change. So we're always interested to know how our members prefer to learn and how they learn most effectively. Recently, I was chatting with a group of members on our Digital Lab programme about this. They are all arts and cultural professionals who are using a scrappy approach to their digital marketing and thinking about a variety of ways to attract audiences – from the user experience, to online campaigns, content creation and just simply getting their emails opened.

The topic of podcasts came up. It started as a discussion around how organizations – especially those with tighter budgets and fewer resources – could successfully produce great-quality, content-rich podcasts. But it soon turned to questions like, what makes a great podcast? Do you have a favourite programme? Favourite topics? I wondered, 'Do any of you use podcasts as active learning tools, rather than listening to things like… True Crime… (no judgment)?'

To my surprise, quite a few said yes. While they often saw it as a mine of random (though funny and interesting) information, many of them also used podcasts as an active engaged learning too. Some of them (cue honest, though seemingly shameless plug) said they listened to Daniel's podcast routinely.

Interestingly, people seemed to really like listening to podcasts on topics they already had some knowledge of. It reassured them. It made them feel confident about the work they were already implementing but inspired to try a few new things. And there *is* something comforting about returning week after week to the warm, friendly embrace of your favourite podcaster. So I think it's good to bear in mind that the content doesn't all have to be ground-breaking stuff. From my experience, podcasts on familiar topics provide a reassuring touchpoint for learners, as much as radical new ideas might inspire new thinking.

For me, podcasts have taken over quietly. They seem to be an underground, 21st-century movement. Everybody seems to be listening to them but it's a solitary activity that only sees the light of day when a conversation is flagging: that terrifying moment when you can masterfully say, 'I was listening to this podcast the other day and *did you know. . . ?*' A totally useful tool to fend off awkward British silences, usurping our faithful weather chat.

Crucially, the number one reason everyone said they love podcasts is the ability to listen whilst doing something else. Everybody knows that it feels positively sacrilegious nowadays to have any time-draining gaps in your daily life. A podcast can turn a seemingly mundane activity (for me that's washing up) into a creative space, an inspiration opportunity… or a learning experience. The gaps between that which we call 'living' – those gaps like commuting, ironing, washing up – those are the moments we love to fill with a podcast. The feeling among our members definitely seems to be, if I can learn during my hour-long ironing pile, why wouldn't I?

Reference

Brand definition

American Marketing Association Dictionary (2018) Definition of brand [online] http://marketing-dictionary.org/

Defining your content plan and using content calendars

We started by talking about the importance of understanding the value proposition and personality of our podcast, the role podcasts take in forming part of our digital branding, as well as understanding our target audience and their user journey. With all this in mind, we then have a great framework for starting to build our content and episode plans. This is fairly straightforward for interview, discussion and information podcasts. For real-life story-based podcasts this may be less obvious, but you still need to understand what are the key elements of a story that people are interested in. For fiction-based podcasts, this process is less relevant, but it can still help you find ideas for your narratives.

Informing your content plan

Before we start any podcast content planning, we need to start by listening. We need to understand what our audience is interested in and passionate about in order to inform our approach in providing value. There is a wide range of 'listening' or 'monitoring' tools, which will be discussed below. Understanding how and what someone searches for can also help inform our understanding of what their needs and interests are.

Using search to inform content themes

Google Trends is a fantastic free tool that allows us to see how users search in Google – and the trends that show over time. The great thing about this tool is that not only can we understand search trends but we can use this to inform our podcast content. We look at this tool in more detail when we look at landing pages, but here we use it to find out what people are interested in, in order to inform what we should be talking about on our social platforms.

In the screenshot shown in Figure 10.1, looking at the word 'jobs' we can start to see a clear seasonal trend. The peak in searches every year is in January, when many of us have new year's resolutions and decide to look for a new job. This tapers off as we get back to work, and then many of us go on our summer vacation and get fired up again about looking for a new job. We then realize that Christmas is just around the corner and think we'll leave it to the new year. And this pattern carries on year after year! In the last four years, due to the global financial crisis, more people have been looking for jobs and therefore searching. Finally, we can see a huge increase in searches for 'jobs' in October 2011. Why? Because Steve Jobs (former CEO of Apple) died, and it creates a skew in our results because of the amount of people searching for his surname.

The Google Trends tool, as standard, will show you relative search volume over time for a particular word or phrase. We can drill down by time, region, country or language. The tool tries to identify related news stories at points on the graph and shows us geographical interest and the most popular and fastest-rising variations of these search terms. Probably the most important feature is the ability to compare the trends for different search terms, and this is particularly important for informing content.

One thing to be clear on is that Google Trends shows you relative volumes of searches, not the actual numbers of searches. If you want the actual number of searches, you'll need to use the Google Ads Keyword Planner tool. Relative volume will show a word at a score of 100 at its highest volume of searches and the rest of the score is relative to this. When multiple words are compared, the highest point given a 100 score is the most-searched word being compared at its highest search volume.

These trends can inform us of what we should be speaking about in our podcast, when we should speak about it, and using what phrases and words. If people are interested in jobs and changing their life in January, that's when we should be speaking about related topics, for example.

Figure 10.1 Google Trends searches for the word 'jobs'

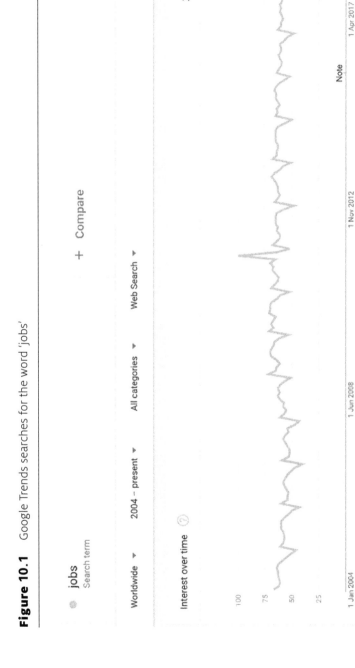

Another phenomenally useful search tool for planning podcast content is AnswerThePublic.com. This tool brings together all of the auto-suggest data from Google and Bing (the phrases that are suggested in the search engines when you start typing), so you can enter a subject and see what the most commonly searched phrases related to it are. What's fantastic, though, is that it brings together all of the questions on the topic into a visualization, so you can see the types of questions people are asking in relation to this topic. Each of these questions could form a podcast episode in their own right, or you can use them to craft elements of an episode. Either way it's a great insight into what the audience really wants to understand.

Social listening tools

Social listening tools are something that every organization of every size should be using. They allow you to monitor a number of different social channels to look for activity around certain phrases or topics. This capability can be used at a number of stages throughout social media campaigns and is essential for effective social media use.

First, these tools can be used in the 'listening' stage, when you are trying to understand what social channels your audience is using, what they are saying, what they are interested in and what your competitors are doing. Many organizations will carry out a listening project before starting any podcast activity, as part of their standard process before planning any content.

Second, these tools can be used to monitor the effectiveness of our podcast activity. We can monitor groups of words and phrases to see what is happening on an ongoing basis, and how our audience reacts to our podcast content.

Finally, social listening tools can be used to manage outreach and engagement by identifying key influencers on social channels. This can be important when trying to grow your audience, but also when dealing with negative feedback or a crisis. The idea is to influence the influencers, much like in traditional PR, but in the case of social media we can do this at a much more granular level.

Some social listening tools also include elements of workflow management, and help you to manage your social media efforts. For example, you may be able to track which social media users you have engaged with, which individual in your organization was involved, and plan future activities.

Social media monitoring and listening tools

There is a huge array of social media monitoring tools out there, varying wildly in price and capability. At the free end of the spectrum you'll find a wide variety of tools; however, these tools are fairly limited, and the old adage that you get what you pay for generally holds true.

The number of paid tools available is dizzying, but I would certainly recommend taking a look at the following:

http://www.brandwatch.com – my favourite social monitoring tool and well worth the cost. Very powerful, flexible and used by some of the world's leading companies.

http://www.mention.com – one of the lower-cost social monitoring tools with a free trial available.

http://www.hootsuite.com – a great social management tool that allows you to do some social monitoring activities, with a free version available.

http://www.howsociable.com – offering a free version and paid-for options, this tool will allow you to benchmark a brand using a number of social metrics.

Social analysis tools

Social analysis tools are different to social listening/monitoring tools in that they generally look at one social platform and give some analysis or functionality for that particular platform. In fact, many social media sites have these built in. For example, Facebook Insights will give you a range of reports that allow you to see which of your posts were most popular, where the users that like you are in the world, and who is engaging with your content.

There are literally thousands of these tools out there. Generally they will analyse your audience and content and provide some insight into how to take your campaigns forward. I have highlighted a few below to give a flavour of what you can expect:

http://www.tweriod.com – find out the most effective time of day and day of the week to post your tweets.

http://klear.com – analyse social influencers with this excellent free tool with premium options.

http://www.followerwonk.com – an oddly named but very powerful tool for analysing Twitter audiences and growing your audience, part of the moz.com set of tools.

Facebook Insights – accessed when you have set up a Facebook page, this lets you know what content is working.

Twitter Analytics – accessed when you are logged into Twitter at analytics. twitter.com, with lots of insights into what has worked and what hasn't.

YouTube Insights – accessed via the social platform itself, it lets you find out which of your videos are actually getting engagement.

The list could go on and on, so we've compiled and are constantly updating a huge list on the website to accompany this book: http://www.targetinternet.com/podcastbook

Analytics

Your web analytics is actually one of the most powerful tools for informing your podcast activity.

We'll explore analytics in more detail in Chapter 24, but it is worth mentioning at this point that analytics can help you understand which of your content and podcast landing pages are most popular.

So, we can use a combination of social media monitoring, search and analytics tools to understand the kinds of things our target audience is interested in. We then need some way of planning this activity into a schedule and getting the most out of it. We'll look at podcasting monitoring in Part Three, but to tie these marketing activities together with our podcast we're going to want to build a content calendar.

Content calendars

A content calendar is simply a document that allows you to plan your content, in this case podcasts, into a schedule. It also allows you to plan any associated marketing activity, such as social posts and emails, as well as making sure you've researched the topic properly and thought about social outreach.

Content calendar template

We have created a content calendar template that you can download, modify and use as you wish. It includes headings for all of the topics below and is a great way to plan your podcast activity:
https://www.targetinternet.com/digital-marketing-podcast-episode-110-digital-marketing-calendars/

Content calendar headings

A good content calendar will help you maximize the impact of your podcast content and bring a number of your digital channels together. Here are the questions a good calendar should cover:

When: What date is this particular podcast going to be published?

Title and description: What's the title and description that will go out with the podcast when it's published?

Landing page URL: Where will the podcast live on our website?

Keywords: Have we done our research and factored in what phrases people use to search for this topic? What are these phrases?

Published: Is it live already?

Social posts: Have we posted to each of the appropriate social channels?

Email: Which email is this podcast going to be promoted in?

Advocates: Who are those people that regularly share our content and leave positive comments that we should get this podcast to?

Influencers: Who are those people that have access to the audience we want that we should get this podcast to and encourage them to share?

Conclusions: Once we have a good understanding of the content we should be recording, and we have planned its distribution, we can then start to iterate. We can learn from our successes and failures and keep improving our content and results.

Driving action from podcasts   11

In many scenarios, we want to drive an action from our podcast listeners. This could be anything from driving a product sale through to driving somebody to get involved in volunteering for a good cause, but we often want action. These 'calls to action' need to be effective, but must also not get in the way of the content. Our prime objective with a podcast is to entertain, engage or educate: everything else is secondary. However, a good podcast will drive brand loyalty and awareness and makes an action a lot more likely.

There are two key scenarios to consider:

Direct action – you use some sort of call to action within the podcast to drive an action elsewhere. Normally that would be on a website or social media, but could also be an app install or a phone call. These actions come in two forms again. The first is a direct drive to your business objective such as a sale or lead generation. More likely, however, is that you simply move somebody along the user journey, not expecting a direct business transaction, and rather get them to sign up for an email newsletter, a free membership or a private group. You then have the opportunity to further engage and drive them toward your business objective later.

Digital branding action – the other scenario that will drive an action is a longer-term build-up of brand awareness, familiarity and preference. Basically, you want people to become aware of what you do, to trust you, and at some point in the future for them to seek a product or service from you at a time where they have a requirement.

In this chapter we want to briefly look at your direct action options:

Introductory sponsorship message. This sets the scene of who has brought the podcast to the audience and starts building a relationship. Although no direct action is given, it starts the conversation for later.

Content discussions. These are low-key mentions within the content, at relevant moments, of things the audience could seek out online, such as new products or services, downloadable content, newsletters or groups. They should not be 'pushy' sales messages and should only be included when relevant.

Midroll sponsor messages. These are much like ads, but add to the content by providing their own narrative with some form of call to action that offers value. For example, 'And now a message from our sponsor', leading to a piece of content in its own right.

Favour ask. If your podcast has low commercial content and you have built a rapport with your audience, you can directly ask for a 'favour' from your audience to take a look at something or to carry out an action. However, if you do this too much you'll 'burn' your trust.

Post-roll direct call to action. The end of the podcast is the ideal time to be more directly commercial and a sales message is acceptable; after all, the listener can leave at any point now. If you've provided enough value via your content and built trust, people will listen.

Show notes. The landing pages for your podcast can offer huge amounts of value such as listing links, offering downloads and signing up for exclusive content.

Community. These calls to action encourage listeners to join some form of online community such as a private Facebook or LinkedIn group. You can also use real-world events in the same way.

The key to driving action from your podcast is not going in too hard, building trust first and providing value. At this point you can then drive a listener to a next step, rather than going straight in for a sale. Focusing on content in the podcast and then building additional content and communities in different channels and formats is the key to driving your user to the next step.

Part Three
Building your podcast and making it a success

The importance of landing pages and show notes (and getting SEO right)

Whether you are just starting your podcast, or already have some episodes published, growing your audience is one of the number one priorities for every podcaster. Naturally, after all the hard work you've put into publishing podcast content, you want listeners to find your show. Making your content extra consumable and findable is what this chapter is all about.

A supporting website

To make your podcast easy to find online, you will need to have web pages that support your show. There are a few ways worth exploring to approach where these web pages live. You can give your show its own website, or you could choose to create your podcast-supporting web pages as a section within your company or brand website. For most independent podcasters you will want a dedicated website for your show, but for brands or organizations creating content to support their day-to-day business activities, building your show into your existing site makes perfect sense.

Most podcast hosting services will provide you with essential web page publishing services. Typically they will all provide you with a functional blogging-type platform that is easy to set up and where you can publish a new web page for each episode you publish. You can usually also add in additional pages of support content such as an 'About Us' page and

'Contact Details'. Working with a podcast host's publishing solution is a great place to get started as they are designed with podcasters in mind. If you are not familiar with web page publishing, we would recommend reading through your hosting provider's help pages for their publishing platforms and keeping things simple. Don't fall into the trap of over-complicating everything related to getting your show live. Web page design and ongoing support can be a huge distraction and drain on your time. Our advice every time is to keep things simple and get started; there will be time to fine-tune and refine stuff once you get going. If you are more confident with publishing web pages and you want more functionality and design control for your show's website then, of course, you don't have to use the built-in web publishing functionality, but for many shows, it is a great place to get started.

Placing your podcast content onto any website

Podcast hosting companies will provide you with an embeddable player for each episode you publish. It sounds fancy we know, but an embeddable player is just a clever piece of webpage code which, once placed into any web page, gives users of that page the ability to play, pause, fast-forward or rewind an episode. These embeddable players can be placed onto any web page or blog post created to house each episode of your show. You can host your podcast episodes on a dedicated podcast hosting solution, but by using the embeddable player you can then feature episode audio content on any web pages you manage. No special connections or software are required to hook up your audio content on one service with your website hosting elsewhere – just make use of your embeddable player.

Creating your own stand-alone fully customized show website

If you want to have complete control over how your show website looks and functions then opting for a custom website build is the way to go. Just be aware that you will be significantly adding to the overall cost and time involved in launching your show. Many online platforms can make setting up a customized website easier but to be honest, if you want something quick and functional check out your podcast hosting company's offerings first. They are custom built for a podcaster's needs and come without the extra hassle and expense of an entirely new and separate website hosting package.

A web page for every episode

Regardless of where your podcast website is placed, each time you publish a new show, you will want to create a new page for that episode. These new episodes should ideally be pulled into the index for your show but will exist as separate pages in their own right. Some platforms, particularly those focused around blogging, will call these 'new posts', some 'new pages'. Don't get too hung up on the terminology. The key take-home is that every episode needs to have its own separate home on your website. You want to avoid having one page where you post up every new show. It's fine if your index page pulls in a summary of each episode as you post, but just be sure that you can click on that summary and be taken to a separate page with its own web address where just that one episode's details are provided and where just that one show can be played. Why is that so important? Well, because it makes your shows easier to find in the search engines. We will explore what search engines love a bit later in this chapter. For now, let's focus a bit more on what your episode pages need to include.

A good index page

Every good webpage home for a podcast needs a good show index page. Your show index page is just a web page where all of your episodes are easily accessible. Think of it as a blog, but with your episode audio content built into each post. Typically, like a blog, your show index page will show your most recent shows at the top, with older shows appearing lower down the page. The page will give a title, episode number and summary of content for each show together with an embedded episode player with player controls. Each show summary can also include some form of artwork to help to distinguish the content of that show if that works with your overall design, but it isn't essential if you want to keep things simple.

A helping hand with your show notes

Some shows will go to the trouble of recording the time points in each episode where important subjects, sections or information are shared. Time stamping your show notes is a lot of additional work and takes time to do manually but there is a shortcut that can help. There are a lot of online transcribing services that charge by the minute. You send them your audio files and a few days later you get sent a typewritten transcript of everything that is said, with timestamps on when it was said. That's fine for short audio snippets, but when you have a 60- or 90-minute episode, the cost per minute can soon add up. We have been playing with an online transcription service called Temi.com. Their system uses artificial intelligence to transcribe your audio and does it lightning fast. Providing the sound quality is good, and the accents of those participating are not too hard to interpret, it does quite a good job. It makes quite a few errors, but they only charge 10 cents a minute, so an hour-long show can be roughly transcribed for $6, which we think is excellent value. You can try out the service for free on their website, so check it out and see if you think it could help you with making show notes for your episodes.

See www.temi.com

Multiple ways to consume

In addition to your embeddable player, it's essential that you link to any of the services through which listeners can subscribe to your content. Apple Podcasts, Google Podcasts, Spotify and many others all make it easy for listeners to subscribe to your show and automatically download any new audio content you produce. Each of these networks will have a recommended badge or link format for you to use. Make sure you have taken note of the look and function of these links; getting these links wrong can set you at a disadvantage with those networks. For example, many listeners will listen and subscribe to your show through Apple's iTunes software. Your show may well be listed in the iTunes Store, so you may think that a link from something that says 'listen in iTunes' might be a great idea. Apple doesn't see it like that. They stipulate you should use the term 'Listen on Apple Podcasts'. They even provide a graphical badge you can use for the purpose. Referencing iTunes instead of Apple Podcasts might make more sense to your audience, but it's a big black mark against you as far as Apple is concerned and makes it very unlikely that they would ever feature you as a featured podcast within iTunes. Learn how each of the networks likes to play ball and follow their guidance on graphical usage, logos, names and branding. Getting this right helps to get your relationship with them off to a good start.

Understanding what people search for

Having an understanding of the common questions and queries people ask around the subject covered by your podcast episode can be a real help in knowing how to approach search engine optimization of your show episode pages. One tool we absolutely love for helping with this is called AnswerThePublic. This website-based tool will ask you for a topic or subject area you want to explore. Be sure to hang around and take your time asking that all-important first question. Their video character 'The Searcher', who greets you on the first page of the site, gets more and more impatient if you keep him waiting, which is partly worth a visit in itself. Type it in and it will give you back all the common questions and searches around that phrase people commonly ask in search engines like Google, Bing and YouTube. Truly, it's a treasure trove of information. We have even turned to this to get initial ideas on the sorts of questions we should cover and answer in advance of recording a show. Go on... stop reading now and give it a go. It's so fab you can lose ages marvelling at all the insights and data it sends you back so don't spend too long there. There is lots more we still need to share with you.

See www.answerthepublic.com

Search engine optimization

Search engines like Google and Bing are great, aren't they? They index billions of web pages so that when you type in a keyword and hit 'Search', you get a quick summary of hopefully the best content on the web that could help with answers to your search. Search engines do this by regularly index-ing billions of individual web pages and making a note of what each web page is about. They also take a look at hundreds of other factors they can measure, like how many other web pages link to a specific web page, and how many pages link to all those pages that link to an individual web page. It's mind-boggling in its complexity and huge books have been written on the art and science behind search engine optimization of web page content. As a podcast producer, you don't need to get too hung up on all that complexity, but a short primer on the basics and how they might relate to how you structure podcast content is useful.

Why one page is never enough

Let's suppose that we create one single web page and post details of each podcast episode into that page as we go. It's simple enough to do. Just keep updating that one page with details of each show added to the top and hey presto we have one page that does everything we want. The problem with this approach is that the search engines will visit that one page and look at all the episodes and try to work out what keyword searches your one page is most relevant for. The more show episodes you add, the more confused the search engine is going to get about what that one page is actually about. It is unlikely the search engine will conclude that your multi-angled page is more about any of the subjects it covers than other pages that focus on one specific topic and have a clear focus.

So it's essential that each show has its own web page or post because it helps search engines to properly index and understand each page of your website. You get a lot more visibility within the search rankings this way. The ideal outcome is that each web page or post that makes up your show gets indexed and appears for different phrases. People will start to find individual episodes because they searched on a particular topic and that individual episode page was relevant and showed up for their search. If they enjoy the episode, they might listen to a few more or, even better, subscribe and get all your podcast content automatically downloaded.

Landing pages

In web publishing terms, any web page designed to be a first port of call for a new website visitor is known as a landing page. For podcasters, each new show web page becomes a new potential landing page where new listeners/website visitors can land on and start the journey to becoming regular content consumers.

Let's explore how to make any one of these landing pages even more attractive to the search engines and people searching for them. When I type in any keyword into a search engine, I get a page of results sent back to me. These returned results are called Search Engine Result Pages or SERPs. When you look at any SERP, you will see there are some paid-for ads at the top of the page and then some other listings not marked with the term 'ad' below these. These listings not marked as ads are organic search results, and they are what we are trying to make use of if we SEO our content.

Optimizing your landing pages for search engines

If you look at each of the organic listings in the SERPs, you will see they all have a fixed format. There will be a title which is highlighted in underlined blue type (typically around 60 characters) and then a web address and a short description of the page. The descriptions shown vary in length but generally are between 120 and 160 characters. Search engine users scan these results quite quickly to work out which listing will most likely give them the best solution to their needs.

How to control web page titles and descriptions

The great news is that you can have quite a bit of control over what these titles and descriptions say. Search engines encourage web designers to make use of special code elements called meta tags to provide additional information about each web page. These meta tags won't be seen by web users, but if you look at the raw code of a web page like a search engine does they are very easily found. Search engines use these meta tags to populate all their SERP pages. There are lots of different hidden meta tags a web page might make use of, but the essential ones for search engines are the meta title and meta description tags. You can't guarantee the search engine will always use the meta title and meta description tags of your web pages. Sometimes the search engine will have a go at writing its own listings based on what it sees on the page but in our experience, more often than not, it's the meta tags that get used if they have been provided.

A 'meta-tastic' tool

If you want a great tool to read your meta titles and descriptions, check out the MozBar browser plugin for Chrome. This free plugin makes it really simple to read all the meta tags on any webpage you visit using your browser. Just click on the 'page inspect' icon in the top left-hand side of your browser and you can see how the meta titles and description for that page are set up. It's great for your own pages, but also handy to see how other website owners are crafting theirs.

Fine-tuning the promise of every web page with meta tags

The secret to driving more traffic to your website is to handcraft the meta title and meta description for each episode page to make them as enticing as you can. Most web publishing platforms will give you access to edit meta tags within their publishing controls. If you are not sure how to edit your web pages' meta tags, speak to your website designer or hosting provider and they will be able to point you in the right direction.

We like to think of the title and description as offering the promise of what the user will get if they click on the listing. It's the promise behind the click. Try to keep your meta tag content short, factual and to the point. Try to answer, 'What's in it for me if I click on the link?' Teasing people in with a key question answered by your content, or leveraging on that episode's guest expert are both techniques that work well in our experience. Look at the way other web pages in the SERPs use their titles and meta descriptions to communicate their own 'promise behind the click', then try to better their efforts. Try as much as you can to keep the title factual and strongly aligned to the keyword phrase that someone searching for that episode might search on. And always keep it honest and genuine. Simply lying and then not delivering when the user gets to your page isn't something users or the search engines will tolerate. If you create copy that does entice users to click, and the user doesn't end up back on the search engine seconds later performing an additional search, the search engine is going to start to take notice of this incredibly clickable solution to its users' questions. When they see a page they served up getting clicks, that page can quite quickly rise up through the ranks to surface closer to the top and be placed in front of more and more people who click. As more people find and love your content, so they are more likely to link to it or share it with others, which search engines also clock and note in your favour. This is somewhat of an oversimplification of how search engines actually rank content, but the click-through rate and user reactions to your content are definitely known key factors for what ranks in search engines. So when publishing your web pages, make them more clickworthy by making full use of your meta titles and descriptions.

Podcasting toolbox additions

Automated transcriptions: Temi.com

Answer the Public: www.answerthepublic.com

Moz Toolbar for Chrome: moz.com/products/pro/seo-toolbar

Defining your podcast audience and content 13

Defining your podcast audience and content is a crucial stage for developing your show. Trying to be all things to all people has traditionally always been highlighted as a recipe for failure, and it's no different with podcasting. It's hard to grow an audience if your content is too general. Before you zoom off in a fit of new-found enthusiasm and start to produce your recordings and podcast episodes, it's well worth taking the time to actually think and imagine who your audience is and what sort of content they would find useful or entertaining. Remember that for everyone who isn't a friend or family member you are another stranger with a microphone who they have no interest in or relationship with. You need to pique their interest and indicate that you are interesting and worthy of their time – and the way to do this is with a well-thought-out audience and a good idea of the sort of content that audience would enjoy.

Finding your niche and sticking to it

If you have never taken the time to clearly define who your audience is you might think that this gives you a free rein to cover anything you want, but that's a mistake. You can't have one without the other. It's a proverbial chicken-and-egg-type relationship. You can't plan out content if you don't know who your audience will be, and you can't gain that audience if you haven't planned out the type of content they will want. Defining your intended podcast audience will help you to create the right content to engage that audience. For the podcaster just starting out, there is a fantastic opportunity to reach out to a niche audience and make the kind of material that audience is hungry for. Don't assume that niche means small in a global marketplace. Good niche content can gain large and loyal followings in the podcasting space and often it's these more focused niche shows that achieve success quickly. It's so much easier to craft the right content when your audience is clearly defined.

Market research your niche

ListenNotes.com

Once you have identified your audience, it's a great idea to do some market research on what other podcast content is out there for that audience. You can do this on any podcast directory, but ListenNotes.com is a dedicated podcast search engine that is excellent for this purpose. You can type in any keyword search, and it will search for episodes or podcasts that cover that topic. It also includes links to subscribe and listen to each show. The service also links to each show's social media profiles and show host contact details if available, so it can also be used for reaching out for guests you would like to feature.

Snap decisions

Podcast listeners are not short of other shows to choose from. When they first come across your show in a podcast directory such as Apple Podcasts, they will make a snap decision on which shows appeal to them. Most audio show formats will be at least 15–20 minutes in length, which in digital media terms is a big ask of time from a consumer. If you haven't taken the time to identify your audience and produce content that will appeal to them, then you will really struggle to acquire new listeners. The more specific you can be the better.

Few listeners are likely to invest the time and trouble of downloading or subscribing to a show that hasn't thought its focus through. 'Podcast host/ hosts speak randomly about stuff' generally isn't a great strategy to grow a loyal audience. You need to have a good idea of why it's going to be relevant to your audience to listen to your show. The all-important question every podcast listener has on their mind is, 'What's in it for me if I listen to this show?' If you haven't defined who your audience will be, and what sort of content would be of interest to that audience, then you are always going to struggle to come up with a good title for your show that speaks to your audience. Once the title has piqued their interest, you need a good one- or two-line pitch to hook them in enough to take an initial listen.

Pitching your show

For the *Digital Marketing Podcast*, we chose a name which very clearly frames the sort of content and audience we wanted to attract. We agonized over the name a fair bit when we first started refining our content ideas. At the time in 2012, 'Internet marketing' was a common term being used in the UK for our subject area. There were already a number of established podcasts relating to internet marketing. 'Digital marketing' was a relatively new term. Being digital marketers, we turned to a great free tool by Google called Google Trends. You can use Google Trends to get a good idea of how popular certain phrases are or not. It's perfect for getting an idea of what terms audiences en masse are searching for on Google. When we launched in June of 2011, you can see from Figure 13.1 that 'digital marketing' as a term had recently overtaken 'internet marketing' in the UK. We could see that the general trend of usage for that term was gradually increasing and so it seemed like the right title phrase to back. It could have gone either way of course, but as you can see from the overall trend of usage, we backed the right term.

As well as helping to define your content, identifying your intended audience will also help you to create great content. When reaching out to potential guests for your show, it really helps to have boiled down your show's concept and target audience so that they can really understand how what they could contribute might fit in. Until you are a popular show, your podcast name or branding is unlikely to open many doors. A well-defined and clear mission statement for your show could really help to open doors for you with guest speakers for your show.

Theory into practice

When it came to outlining our content we had a clear audience in mind. We wanted to reach an audience of professionals and business people interested in marketing who were keen to understand and learn about digital marketing. Here was our initial pitch to the world when we started.

Initial show pitch

The Digital Marketing Podcast

The *Digital Marketing Podcast* aims to be a guide to the latest digital marketing news and tools, along with some practical advice from our own day to day use of digital marketing (TargetInternet.com, 2011).

Over the years as we have grown, we have refined this initial pitch, but it's still largely the same and has served us well.

Our current show pitch

The Digital Marketing Podcast

The *Digital Marketing Podcast* combines interviews with global experts, together with the latest news, tools, strategies and techniques to give your digital marketing the edge. Perfect for your daily commute, the podcast aims to be both entertaining and informative (TargetInternet.com, 2018).

Stay focused and true to your audience

Having defined who you want to reach and hooked in an audience with a strong content pitch they couldn't possibly refuse, it's essential to keep your audience in front of mind as your show develops. Your show name and an initial pitch is a promise to your audience. Try to think of it as contractual. If you start to push out other content which isn't of interest to the audience you initially pitched for, then you are going to lose them quickly. When you first start out it's easy to get sidetracked with other topic areas you find interesting, but you must always focus on what your audience is after. There is one golden rule every podcast show producer should keep top of mind when planning their content: podcasting is not about you, it's always about your audience. They are the point. Respect that rule and work tirelessly to give your audience ever better content. Do this and your audience should grow in size and loyalty. Ignore it, and you will disappoint your audience and fail to gain the success all your hard work and dedication deserves.

Figure 13.1 Internet marketing vs digital marketing search data trends over time

(Google and the Google logo are registered trademarks of Google Inc, used with permission.) Google Trends, 2018 (https://www.google.com/trends)

Understanding and selection of different podcast formats 14

One of the most important considerations for any new podcaster is selecting a format for their show. Choosing an overall show format can really help to get things moving in the right direction. One of the best bits of advice we can give you would be to listen to a variety of shows that make use of different formats so you can get a feel for what you think might work for you and the content ideas you have for your podcasting efforts. When we started the *Digital Marketing Podcast*, our main purpose was that the show would mirror something that was already happening. We would have been meeting up semi-regularly to share stories and tips of our digital travels; we both looked forward to these catch-ups and always learned lots from each other. We hoped that by adopting this as a format for our show, it would really help to keep the content real and natural. Over time we have mixed things up, including formats like interview shows, multiple hosts and roundtable discussions, but our core premise of two guys talking about stuff they love still remains the most popular element of our show. Trying to categorize podcasts is a tricky thing to do.

The podcast format has an almost infinite number of possible arrangements; it is one of the great joys of the medium. However, our aim with this chapter is to inspire you to explore different formats and possible arrangements. The possible subject and style options you can choose from are vast, but great podcasting starts with one simple thing all shows have in common: voices. In this exploration we have based our categorization of different show types around how different voices can be organized and leveraged upon to communicate the show. We hope this will inspire you to identify a format that will suit your purposes.

Solo show

The solo show format is the audio podcasting equivalent of a talking head. It's one of those formats some people do really well, but if you've ever tried to do it, you've probably realized it's easy to run out of steam.

Solo podcasting works best when the podcast host can explore a particular content focus that they have a lot of knowledge or confidence with. Without a co-host or guest, there really isn't anyone else to spark ideas and questions off to move the episode forward. Although solo shows can appear to be one long monologue (and we know of some podcasters who can literally grab these in one take with some well-planned-out thoughts), in reality, you have the benefit of being able to edit together several different sections if you do stutter or run out of steam. Just be sure to keep the audio consistent by recording in the same place with the same equipment so you can easily edit it together and hide any necessary joins.

The fact that you're the only person required to create the content is also one of the most significant benefits of the solo format. Solo podcasters have the freedom of managing their own schedule, and therefore the luxury of shoehorning in a new episode as the schedule allows. And as a regular publishing schedule is so important to grow an audience for your show, the solo show format is definitely worth exploring and giving a go.

You are never alone

We often explain to people who we are signing up to be guests on our show that the interview we are about to record will be quite relaxed and informal, like a casual chat down the pub or at a coffee shop. The difference is that we need to remember that there are between 6,000 and 8,000 people sat right next to us listening in. Although your audience doesn't take a speaking role in your show, they are actively participating and engaging with what is going on. You can't see it, but as they listen they will be smiling, laughing, frowning, occasionally maybe getting confused, or worse, getting distracted and fidgeting. No one wants to be introduced to a social situation where others form a closed, niche group and exclude newcomers. So, regardless of what format arrangement you have adopted, always be mindful of your audience and take every opportunity to ensure they understand what just happened or is about to happen. Even solo is never truly solo: you always bring passengers.

When you create each episode, make sure you have plotted in some detail your route through the particular topic you are covering. The stronger your overall connection with the shape of the content, the better your solo performance will be, and that takes planning, detailed knowledge and a bit of practice to pull off effectively. When starting out, a well-plotted route will help you to keep the podcast content moving forward, which will help to keep the audience engaged and on track with where you are in the journey you are taking. The last thing you want is to end up lost in your own topic of conversation or not really having enough of interest to say. Try to avoid your show becoming one where someone talks about whatever comes up in their head at that moment. A randomly generated stream of consciousness that isn't planned rarely works as well as the author thinks it does and it usually struggles to retain an audience's interest. The best solo shows have structure and an excellent narrative direction, so plan ahead before you dive in! If you listen to a few good examples, you will find that the solo host often follows the tried-and-tested formats employed for an engaging conference speech or solo presentation. They introduce the overall topic and give a flavour of the key areas they will be exploring, and then signpost each section of that exploration as they go. Ultimately, all paths lead to key learning or revelation at the end.

Solo show examples

Seth Godin's Startup School by Seth Godin: art19.com/shows/startup-school

TED Talks Daily by TED: www.ted.com/talks

Narrative storytelling

Storytelling techniques can also work well as solo podcast performances and in fact are so commonly employed that they form a show format category all of their own. The nature of oral storytelling lends itself to the solo podcast but with one key difference from a live performance: you cannot actually see your audience. You can't take questions from them or see what's igniting their interest and what isn't. For this reason, it's a good idea to practise these skills at any given opportunity and master storytelling in front of a live audience, if you can, to learn the art and the craft.

A lot of practitioners of narrative storytelling enhance their content with background music and audio effects to add ambience and experience, mainly when dealing with fiction. Doing this adds to the amount of post-production you will need to perform on your recordings, but if you have the confidence and the skills, it can be a fun addition to the show. The critical thing to focus on is that any such post-production should enhance the storytelling rather than stand out as a thing all on its own. Less is more. Keep it subtle and don't overdo it; the story always needs to be the star of the show. For business podcasts, there is a lot you can learn from some of the masters of live audience storytelling recorded via TedTalks. We have yet to find a lousy presenter on a TED talk – and this comes from a lot of planning, practice and knowing the subject inside out. Watch them and learn the craft. Our final tip for anyone choosing this format is to keep a very close eye on audience drop-off rates in your Apple podcast connect account. It's a sure sign you are not engaging the audience enough and need to work on your content and technique.

> **Narrative storytelling podcast examples**
>
> **Lore** by Aaron Mahnke: www.lorepodcast.com
>
> **Hardcore History** by Dan Carlin: www.dancarlin.com/hardcore-history-series/

The two-host format

Two people who know each other well and are passionate about a topic is, in our opinion, a bit of a magic formula for an excellent business podcast. You get the added advantage of two personalities who can interact but with fewer of the technical and scheduling headaches of having multiple hosts.

Establishing roles very early on for each host can really help to refine your on-air rapport. For the *Digital Marketing Podcast*, when we do a two-host format recording, I (Ciaran) usually take the role of being the newbie who is probing and exploring a topic with Daniel, who usually takes the part of the subject expert. This happened quite naturally, but recognizing it worked, we kept it. As it happens, I got into podcasting and digital marketing by listening to an early show Daniel started around 15 years ago called *Internet Marketing*. Daniel was my go-to expert for a full two years before I actually met him. When I finally got the chance to work with him, it was also the perfect opportunity to pick his brains on all manner of subjects. Some I knew very well, others were entirely new to me. Either way, I found that by playing the novice, not only did I always learn more, but it also helped to ensure that our audience could learn and develop their knowledge. Very occasionally you will hear Daniel reverse these roles when he knows I have something to share. These moments usually occur as a result of our pre-show catch-up where we plan out what we are going to talk about and knock together a plan of approach. Over time we have both developed podcasting personas and an on-air relationship that we share with our listeners just as any group of friends would do.

Two-host examples

Libsyn's The Feed by Libsyn with Elsie Escobar and Rob Walch: thefeed.
  libsyn.com

Screw the Nine to Five by Jill Stanton and Josh Stanton:
  www.screwtheninetofive.com/

Interview shows

The interview show has to be one of the most widely adopted formats in podcasting. It is how I (Ciaran) started out in podcasting – my first three podcasts followed the host with a different interviewee each episode. Typically, you have a regular host who interviews different experts or specialists in the subject area of the podcast.

Using this format, you will find that as you introduce topics or show guests, you develop the skill of working with and editing your own voice (so it's actually an excellent stepping stone to exploring the solo show format). Again, the key to a good interview show is plotting out your route in advance and sharing that with the person you are interviewing. There is never a shortage of experts you can invite onto your show when you start looking. Authors always have new books they want to promote, and leading experts or entrepreneurs still have new angles or project areas they are keen to share with a broader audience. But you don't have to limit yourself to the main-stream superstars – look around you at the people and organizations you meet every day. It's likely many of them could be a potential guest or be connected to a potential guest who could make a significant and fascinating interviewee. In most cases, you just need to ask.

Good interview shows need proper planning. It takes time to recruit your guests, agree on a topic, plan out a structure that will work and schedule in the recording. Again, as a regular schedule of publishing is so important, we cannot stress enough the importance of planning ahead. Good interviews rarely happen entirely off the cuff.

Interview show examples

Ologies by Alie Ward: www.alieward.com/ologies/

Masters of Scale by WaitWhat LLC With Reid Hoffman: mastersofscale.com

---

Multiple show hosts

While technically two is a multiple-host format, for the sake of clarity we are going to classify this as more than two because the dynamics of this kind of show are slightly different and need to be understood.

A multiple-host show can be incredibly engaging if you get a good mix of characters who all get on and work well with each other. There is a bit more scope in a multiple-host format for different show hosts to go off at a tangent when recording, so again, prior planning and structure are key to making this format work. Spontaneous digressions are fun, but you also need to keep things moving forward to a meaningful and logical conclusion. This means planning. Quite detailed planning actually, which all the show hosts need to be aware of. You typically need to have a good idea of who will be taking centre stage for different parts of the show, and you will need your hosts to prepare for their contribution in advance to avoid too much general backchat and infilling. Occasional fun and random digressions can be great but respect your audience enough to quickly get back on track to cover what your show title and premise have promised.

In any group, it's easy for in-jokes to develop or well-known facts within that group to be taken as read. This is fine for those in that group, but for any outsiders, these things come across as cliquey. If this is a significant portion of your podcast audience, you are going to hit problems. Always try to remember that the podcast audience is effectively in that room with you and trying to follow everything that's being said. Your audience won't be party to what your plan is for that episode's content and won't have the benefit of knowing like you all do what is coming up next, so it's important to help them and manage their expectations of where proceedings are going. It helps them to stay in the room with you all and be a part of the fun. To avoid any audience alienation it's a good idea for someone in the group to take on the role of grand host, keeping the direction of the show on track, giving an overall sense of where you are going in that episode and explaining or exploring any references your audience might not be up to speed with. Try to assume you have new members of the team sat in on every recording and make sure they are fully part of what happens. Balancing the need to explain while also keeping the episode moving forward will get easier as you all become more practised.

One of the challenging aspects of a multiple-host show is that you all need to be able to regularly get together to record content. We know how hard that is with just two of us, so don't underestimate how quickly it becomes the age-old headache of trying to herd cats when you have three or more show hosts you need to get together regularly. The physical process of capturing good-quality audio from multiple show hosts also presents a few challenges, so potentially this might be a format you would want to one day progress towards or experiment with at a later date rather than starting out with it from day one.

Multiple-host show examples

My Dad Wrote a Porno by Jamie Morton, James Cooper and Alice Levine: www.mydadwroteaporno.com

You, Me and the Big C by Radio 5 Live with Rachael Bland, Deborah James and Lauren Mahon: www.bbc.co.uk/programmes/p0608649

Roundtable/panel discussions

There are obviously a lot of similarities between multiple-host shows and roundtable format/panel discussions. However, the overall format is usually much more locked down with a specific topic or content exploration planned and mapped out. There is far less random chat and much more focused contribution from each of the participants.

Usually this format is an occasional choice rather than a regular arrangement for a show, so participants don't necessarily know each other as well as they would do for a multi-host format. Be sure not to neglect this fact. Each participant in any roundtable discussion will need to be introduced to your audience and the reason for their place at the recording table clearly communicated. Be sure to cover this in the introductory part of the show and, if you can, we always find it helps to get a bit of personality into these introductions. Try to get a useful and relevant angle on all your participants so the audience can build up a picture of who is in the discussion and what they will be contributing. Then, especially if many people are involved, it is important for the host to reiterate and reference who will be speaking by directing questions to particular panellists and perhaps helping the audience further by injecting a reminder on why the directed question is relevant to them and their expertise/work. This can help massively the more panellists you have involved – remember that all the audience have to go on is a voice so don't rely on the initial introductions to be the only signpost for who is talking and why they are the right person to answer or contribute. Signpost all the way!

If you have never hosted a panel before, our advice would be start off small and learn as you go. In our experience fewer voices on a panel work better than too many, so experiment with some small panels of two or three before you build up to a cast of thousands. Very often panel discussions can be included in company or conference events, in which case an experienced panel host may help you manage that process. You just need to work on the challenge of capturing the discussions in a live environment.

Roundtable/panel examples

Do the Right Thing with Danielle Ward, Margaret Cabourn-Smith and Michael Legge: https://www.comedy.co.uk/podcasts/dotherightthing/

Brexitcast with Laura Kuenssberg, Katya Adler, Adam Fleming and Chris Mason: https://www.bbc.co.uk/programmes/p05299nl

There will more than likely be a default format for any podcast that the majority of your content will fit into. However, over time you may want to experiment with a variety of different arrangements. Solo performances, interviews with individuals or even two or three guest participants can be fun additions to your show. Occasionally it can be fun to mix things up by playing with other formats and seeing how your audience responds. Just be sure to take them on that journey with you and explain what you are trying out and why.

Preparing your podcast recording environment 15

Before we talk about technical equipment, we want to share a hidden truth about podcasting with you which should be much more widely understood. The best thing for the quality of the audio you record isn't anything to do with expensive fancy-looking mics and software. For great audio you need to control and understand the environment you record in. For sure the technical equipment can add its layer of polish and finesse, but get the environment wrong and the results you get just won't be that good, no matter how much you have spent on equipment.

Your war on unwanted noise

Obviously you want somewhere quiet, with no distracting noises. Clocks, fridges, pets, street noise, even plumbing and heating or air conditioning can make it into your recording and become a big problem. Computer equipment with all its fans, drives and status alerts can also catch you out so think about steps you can take to silence or remove these factors. When picking your space, you almost need to risk-assess the likelihood of any unwanted sound creeping into your recordings and take what steps you can to minimize them.

For great recording, you want to capture the sound as it happens in a clear and crisp format, so it sounds delicious. The problem is, sound waves like to bounce off hard surfaces and when they do they come back into your microphone and make your audio sound anything but delicious or crisp. Most rooms have lots of hard surfaces to catch you out. Step into any bathroom with all its glass, mirrors and hard tiled surfaces, and you can hear the sound bouncing back and forth in the form of mini echoes. Bathrooms are an extreme location for them, but other rooms have them to varying degrees. The more you can reduce that echo the better and more delicious your recording will generally sound. Sometimes echoes are of course inevitable, like for example a sound recording in a gothic cathedral, but most of the time you will want to do all that you can to minimize them.

Improvisation

Your best friend in the war against echoes is soft furnishings. When we first started out podcasting, any room with lots of soft furnishings was a good bet. We've also found that most modern car interiors have a similar echo-dampening effect, provided you can get the car well away from any traffic noise. There have even been occasions when we have resorted to recording in full closets or even building a wall of coats around our microphone to dampen down the effect of that well-known mecca of hard surfaces, the business conference room.

As fun as this sort of improvising is, there are a few slightly more sophisticated solutions you can opt for. You want to try to arrange your audio recording space so that with the minimum of effort you are ready to go and get recording. The more things you have to get set up, the greater the chance that you will simply fiddle or procrastinate and not get on with the job in hand, especially when you first start. Do yourself a favour and find a suitable space you can record in with minimal disruption and minimal setting up.

Improvised recording spaces

Most of us won't have the luxury of a professional recording studio, but you can make use of the pro studios' secret weapon in the war against poor quality sound: acoustic foam. It's usually black or dark grey and raised in thick triangular peaks or ridges of varying forms. Its effect is to break down and absorb any sound waves that hit it. You can purchase packs of acoustic foam panels and use these to cover hard surfaces in your recording room. Just fix the acoustic foam to any of the hard surfaces in the room and boom, things start to sound delicious. You don't have to cover an entire room. For years Daniel used to record in a foam booth built into a small floor-to-ceiling cupboard in the corner of his office in Brighton. He affectionately referred to the closet as 'Narnia', and it was ideally suited to its use. There was once an occasion when we hadn't been able to book our usual recording studio, so we tried recording together in Narnia. The results were great but to be honest, we both found being huddled into a small cupboard a bit too close for comfort.

If you don't have a small booth or cupboard you can convert into an audio booth, something as simple as a thick curtain drawn around you when recording can make an enormous difference. Setting up a thick curtain and rail around your recording space is one of the easiest ways to make your own recording booth with great acoustics and it's super fast to clear out of the way.

Portable solutions

Another option is a small portable audio recording booth. These come under a variety of different names so try a search for 'Portable Sound Booth' or 'Sound Shield', and you will find some great ready-built options in the £40–£80 price region. They look like curved or C-shaped screens covered in acoustic foam. These effectively place a small curved wall of acoustic foam around your microphone to help dampen reflected sounds from the walls behind your mic and they can significantly help improve audio quality. Just beware of sounds bouncing off hard surfaces behind you as these can still make it into your microphone. You will also need to get quite close to your mic and the foam for these to have the right effect.

Voice-over-IP interviews

If you are wanting to interview guests for your podcast, voice-over-IP call services like Skype are a fantastic time- and travel-saving tool for the busy podcaster. We will explore different voice-over-IP services in more detail in Chapter 16, but we touch on them here because in order to really embrace the benefits they bring, you are going to need to make sure your recording space has a fast and reliable internet connection.

Internet speed matters

If you are recording interviews online, it is essential to do everything you can to ensure you have a good internet connection. If you are lucky and get reliable fast speeds all the time then good for you; however, not every podcaster is so blessed. Internet speeds can drop suddenly for all sorts of complicated and seemingly inexplicable reasons, so it pays to know how to tweak things to your advantage to get you out of a tight spot should one ever occur. When arranging voice-over-IP interviews, a varying internet speed can result in broken-up audio that's painful to listen to and even more painful and time-consuming to try to stitch back together again when you edit.

One of the most effective precautions you can take to avoid speed drops is to get your laptop or computer set up with a hard-wired Ethernet cable connection, so you are physically connected to your internet router rather than using your wireless connection. A hard-wired connection can seriously boost your internet speeds and will certainly minimize the risk of your net connection dropping. How much of a boost will vary but we'd highly recommend you try an internet speed test using your wireless connection and then do the same with an Ethernet cable connection. Try doing a search for 'internet speed test' on Google for a variety of different speed testing options. This fix can more than double the internet speed of even the slowest of broadband services and all for the cost of a few pounds online or at your local computer store. Ethernet cables are amazing.

Understanding internet speeds

Broadband internet speeds are typically measured in 'megabits per second', often shortened to Mbps. 'Bits' are tiny units of data, with a megabit representing a million of them. Services like speedtest.net will measure how fast your connection is – the higher the number of Mbps you have, the speedier your internet connection should be. Just remember that if you share your connection with lots of other users in your office or home, the amount of internet speed available to your machine can drop significantly if other users on your network start downloading large files. Operating system updates, streaming 4K video content, or synchronizing large files with online services like Google Drive or Dropbox can all hog those important Mbps, leaving little for your 'oh so important' interview. If your net connection isn't the spriteliest, do all that you can to minimize these kinds of activity while you record.

Target bandwidth

For a good call experience on any voice-over-IP service, we would recommend aiming at a minimum of 1.5 Mbps upload and download for a one-to-one call. That should give you plenty of bandwidth for both your side of the call and the audio coming from your guest. Some services like Skype will work at much lower speeds but you are more likely to have audio quality problems. Also be aware that if you are going to involve more than one guest on the Skype call you will need to set your baseline slightly higher as each additional participant will consume additional bandwidth. If you only need the audio, turning off the video cameras of everyone on the call can also be a help. It does make communication a little less fluid, but can help to improve your audio.

Managing a guest's remote environment

If you are conducting remote interviews via Skype or a similar service, you will also need to manage conditions at your guest's end to get the best audio. In reality, your options are limited here. You can't expect a guest to go to the lengths you will to get great audio. We have found that it helps to have a pre-call with new guests to talk them through the process of doing the interview. We will look at these pre-calls in more detail in Chapter 18 when we look at using interviews. However, it is worth discussing how you can help to improve your guest's audio environment. We usually ask guests to pick a quiet room with a reliable internet connection. We also advise them to avoid spaces that have lots of echoes.

Headsets or earbuds?

It is well worth asking your guest if they have access to any microphone other than their laptop's internal microphone. Skype headsets can be way better than the laptop's mic, as can the earbuds that come with most smartphones. These earbuds have microphones very similar to those found in laptops, but because they are designed to be positioned much closer to the user's mouth and to pick up close by sounds rather than everything in the room they generally do a pretty good job of capturing the spoken word. Very often guests will have these options lying around their offices and can try them out on your planning call. You can instantly hear how much the sound is improved when they do. Just be careful their ear bud mic doesn't rub against clothing or long hair. Getting these details ironed out in advance of any scheduled interview can go a long way to improving the sound quality you get back.

The double-ender

If you are interviewing another podcaster, the chances are they will be able to help you create a great sound at both ends. In fact, you could try what is known as a double-ender. Double-ender recordings are recorded locally at both ends of the call. Other podcasters can use their set-up, you can use yours, and each of you can create a recording of your half of the conversation. If you are working with a co-host who lives remotely to you, this is an excellent way of capturing your audio. The trick is to make use of a loud sound like a clap or a click that will be picked up by both your microphone and your remote guest's microphone. This will show on the audio timeline of both recordings and gives you a point to line up so that the timings of each conversation match.

Go easy on your guests

Remember your job as a host is to ensure your guest sounds fab. Exploring small things they can do to improve the audio you get back from their end will play a huge part in doing that. Just be sure to explore what they could do easily and don't be too demanding. You want things to stay fun for your guest, not to scare them off with demands or technical barriers. Use what they might have to hand and if that isn't very much it's better to compromise and improvise.

Choosing your recording hardware and software

16

You don't actually need very much equipment to record an audio podcast. You could technically do the whole production from your smartphone end to end, and if you search online, you will find proponents of this minimalist approach. However, it does help to have a little bit more control of the audio you record than what a smartphone on its own can offer. It also helps to be armed with some essential best practice and technical knowledge, so we are going to share with you a few tips we have found that will significantly help improve the quality of your audio productions without breaking the bank. In this chapter there are a number of different tools and online services we are going to share with you. You can find details of where to get each of these tools in the podcasting toolbox at the end of the chapter.

Essential equipment for getting started

To get started you need:

- a laptop capable of running some audio recording/editing software;
- a pair of over-the-ear headphones;
- a USB microphone;
- an inexpensive pop filter;
- some acoustic dampening;
- a space to use this equipment that doesn't have much echo.

This may sound like a very modest set-up if you start to read any of the hundreds of advertorial-based 'how to set up a podcast' articles that proliferate all over the web. Just remember that those articles aim to sell you stuff so they can make money. This book is about getting you podcasting. Quality of audio is important, but you don't necessarily need to spend thousands on your recording equipment to achieve it. Your aim should be to create a recording that is comfortable to listen to when you plug in earbuds and listen on a mobile device. Why should that be your gold standard? Because most podcasts are consumed in this way.

Shelling out

With time and as your audience grows you may well wish to spend on higher-quality audio equipment, but it certainly isn't necessary for starting out. Get set up with the basics and then put your energy and talents into creating engaging content before you really start to shell out on more expensive gear. Modern USB microphones are relatively inexpensive and can give some amazing results if you know how to apply them and set up your recording space as we showed you in the last chapter. With some reasonably low-budget equipment and the right organization, you can achieve great results.

USB microphones

When we first started out, we literally hired a hotel meeting room and purchased a Blue Snowball USB mic for around £75, and that was how we recorded our first few episodes. We still make use of the Blue Snowball for Skype interviews. A good USB mic is a huge leap from the internal mic you will find in most laptops. Laptop mics tend to record all the sound in a room, echoes and all, so for that reason, we would encourage you to avoid them. As a basic recording package, you hopefully already have a laptop with USB ports. Armed with that and a budget USB microphone like the Blue Snowball or Blue Yeti, you have almost everything you need for making great recordings.

Understanding plosives

If you have ever watched video footage of professional singers in a studio audio booth, you will have noticed the mysterious thin circular screen positioned between the singer and the microphone. These black circular discs are called pop filters, and they solve a widespread problem for anyone recording audio in a studio setting. To get great sound from most microphones, you need to be relatively close to the microphone when recording. When we pronounce words with the 'p' or 'b' sound, a small ball of air is projected out from our mouths and will hit any microphone positioned directly in front of us. These small balls of air are technically known as 'plosives'. Try holding the back of your hand within three inches of your mouth and recite 'Peter Piper Picked a Peck of Pickled Peppers'. Feel the force of that air hitting the back of your hand every time you pronounce a P? That's a plosive.

Pop filters

Microphones don't like plosives very much. The force of that air hitting the mic will distort the sound of the recording, producing an annoying popping sound, so steps need to be taken to lessen the effect. You can, of course, aim your voice to the side of the microphone to avoid the popping, but that feels slightly unnatural for most people so we'd recommend using a pop filter as part of your microphone recording set-up. There are two types you can buy. Relatively cheap nylon mesh screens that come with an adjustable positioning arm and clamp (typically under £10). The effect of the nylon is to filter out the plosive which will hit the cloth but not have enough force behind it to then hit the microphone to create any distortion. If you are after something a little more premium than what amounts to a pair of nylon tights stretched over a circle of plastic you can opt for a more beautiful-looking wire mesh pop filter. These have specially angled mesh which cleverly redirects the air away from the mic as you talk through them. Both options work well and will stop popping plosives making it into your recordings, so you decide.

Over-the-ear headphones

A reasonably priced set of over-the-ear headphones are super useful and will enable you to listen to your recordings without outside sounds interfering. If you are recording an interview over Skype, some over-the-ear headphones are essential as they will stop your mic picking up the voice of the person you are interviewing and creating a feedback loop.

What is a feedback loop?

A feedback loop is when sound travels from one speaker back into the mic then out through the other person's speaker and into their mic in a perpetual loop. It results in a loud and uncomfortable high-pitched whistle. These things hurt your ears, so you soon learn to avoid them ever happening by wearing your earphones. We usually encourage the person on the other end of a call to wear earphones as well, but if they don't have any to hand you can help matters by asking them to turn down their speaker volume, so feedback loops are avoided.

Voice-over-IP call interviews

If you want to interview guests for your podcast, there are a large number of excellent voice-over-IP call and video call services you can make use of. Skype is one of the most popular, but FaceTime, WhatsApp, Google Hangouts and services like Zoom are all fantastic time-saving tools. Choosing which service to use will often be something most heavily influenced by your guest. We have made use of a whole bunch of them, but overall we tend to rely on Skype calls as most people we have wanted to interview are familiar with the service, and the quality of the calls is fairly consistent.

You can't beat a face-to-face interview in our opinion, but conducting them takes up a lot of time and effort and can involve many hundreds of miles of travel. Save yourself all that time and expense and do the interview over a suitable voice-over-IP call service. It's usually free to set up an account on these services and the call is free as long as it is delivered using internet-connected devices at both ends.

Software for recording a Skype call

By far the easiest way of recording a Skype call is to make use of audio software designed for that purpose. For Mac users, there are a whole host of software applications that make recording Skype calls easier. Skype now allows you to record audio and video directly within the application, which is great for content producers just starting out. The recorded files are stored online for up to 30 days by Microsoft, so be sure you don't forget to download a copy once your call has finished or you might risk losing the content. In addition to Skype's built-in call recording there are a number of third-party pieces of software that you can use to record calls. If it's just Skype you want to record then Ecamm's Call Recorder for Skype is great. You can record just audio or video calls, and it splits your side and your guest's side of the recording into separate files, which makes things a lot easier to edit. They also have a bolt-on service which works with FaceTime calls.

If you have a Mac and are after something with more features that can record from multiple online voice calling services we highly recommend Audio Hijack by Rogue Amoeba. Again this enables you to record audio from your mic and the sound of your guest via Skype as separate tracks, but its easy-to-use drag-and-drop interface enables you to link up all sorts of different services.

For PC/Windows users we recommend Talkhelper. This is a paid-for package, but they offer a 7-day free trial, with no functionality limitations, that you can try out. The application is able to record both video and audio calls and can store the recordings locally.

A good Skype alternative

As well as Skype, we have also loved using the Zoom web conferencing service. It's actually a fully fledged video conferencing service, but the audio quality is reliable and remains excellent over long distances. Zoom features an audio recording option of any meetings so the call can be recorded without any additional software being needed. We have used this for recording calls to Singapore from the UK with great results. Unlike Skype, your interviewees do not have to have set up an account to take part; you can just send them an invite with a link, and they can join the call. Their free service is limited to just 40 minutes of calls per month but their paid-for service gives you much more generous call allowances for a low monthly fee.

Over-the-phone interviews?

There are many ways podcasters can record phone calls and the internet is not short of complex diagrams and methods for doing so, but one of the easier ways we have found is to purchase some Skype phone credit and interview a guest by calling their mobile phone via Skype. You can then use your Skype recording solution to capture the recording like you would any other Skype call. Now you might think, 'Great – that will make it super easy for my guests to take part'. It does, and it's a useful option if the guest you are trying to interview is in a location that doesn't have internet coverage but does have a good mobile signal. The problem is that telephone-generated audio is of very low quality, so if you can avoid this type of interview, you should. It can, however, be a handy option when you are in a tight spot so we are sharing it with you.

Audio editing

There is a dizzying array of audio editing options for podcasters to choose from and a fair bit of terminology that seems to have sneaked into the space as well. Audio purists and professionals are often big fans of commercial audio editing software offerings like Adobe Audition or Apple's Pro Logic software for editing up your podcast audio. While the feature lists of these packages are impressive, the learning curve in using them is steep, and we usually recommend podcasters start out with something a bit more basic that won't break the bank. The basic set-up you need for putting your show together is multi-track recording and editing functionality that can output good-quality edited files, and that's what we want to focus you on.

There are two main entry points for audio editing software that we recommend. If you are on a Mac, GarageBand, which comes free as part of OSX, is a great option and one that we have always used for producing the *Digital Marketing Podcast*. Audacity is another great audio editing option and it's available for free on Windows, Mac and Linux systems.

Mobile recording on the run

Sometimes you will inevitably need to record in a space where you don't have your full set-up. Face-to-face interviews are great, but you won't always have the luxury of your guests coming to you. More often than not your guest is helping you out with the content, so it is you that needs to travel to them. So it's a good idea to sort out some more portable solutions.

For face-to-face interviews on the fly, you can get some great little Lavalier mic systems that will plug into your smartphone. These can be attached to each person in the discussion and do a great job at capturing a conversation between two people. You can pick up sets for under £20 online, and it's a good starting point for capturing content on the fly. The only drawback with such a solution is that you won't be able to hear the recording as it happens, as your external mics will plug into the 30mm headphone jack. Also, the audio you capture will all be on one soundtrack, which makes editing much less flexible.

If you want to be able to listen to the recording as it happens and have separate volume controls for each participant, then you can't beat a dedicated portable podcast recorder. They also make it much easier to identify distracting background noises the recording picks up that you just wouldn't notice with the naked ear during a recording. For example, air conditioning or traffic noise can both be big background noise generators, as can mics set with a recording level that's slightly too high and picks up a faint background hum or hisses. If you can listen to the recording as you conduct it, you can correct these things.

There are lots of dedicated portable audio recorders on the market, and prices start around the £60–£90 mark. There are several benefits a dedicated portable recorder brings to the sound recording party. Firstly, using them won't drain your smartphone battery or take up space on your phone's limited storage. Portable audio recorders record onto removable SD or mini SD cards. Many of them also come with removable AA batteries so you can always bring enough power with you or purchase some while you are out and about should you need to. They also don't suffer from receiving social media updates, emails or phone calls when you are recording. But the significant feature dedicated audio recorders offer is the ability to listen to your recording as you make it. Take a look at the Zoom H1 or the Tascam DR-05. Both these devices support high-quality built-in stereo microphones and will allow you to listen to your recording as you make it. The quality of sound they record and the detail they will pick up is astonishing; you will start to hear the world in a very different way through these devices. Being able to spot unwanted background sounds and remove them from the original recording really is hugely valuable and will save you a lot of time and stress.

The magic of dual Lavalier mics

Those dual Lavalier mics we mentioned for smartphones can also be plugged into these portable recorders. With this combination you will be able to listen to the recording as it occurs because most portable recorders will have separate 3mm headphone and mic ports. Lavalier mics are great in an interview and make the recording process much less 'in your face'. You'd be surprised how waving a mic around to capture sound between different participants can ruin the moment for those you are interviewing. It's a permanent reminder that this isn't a normal conversation. Also, the more you wave it around the more you will be varying the distance between the mic and the person speaking, which leads to a sound-levelling problem when you come to edit. Lavalier lapel mics can be clipped on and forgotten. Once clipped into place they keep a constant distance between the mic and the person speaking, which gives you nicely consistent sound levels. Just remember you are both physically attached by wires once you have mic'd up. You don't want a great interview to end with either of you wandering off only to be yanked back into an awkward tangle of wires and recording equipment.

Pimp up your portable audio recorder

Most portable audio recorders will do a great job out of the box, but there are additions you can make to your portable kit that make them even better. Microphone windshields are essential if you are ever to try recording outdoors. The built-in mics of your portable recorder are particularly sensitive to the wind, which will hit the microphone and ruin the recording with a tell-tale roar. Placing a foam or furry windshield over the mic will help to stop this (you can purchase these online for your audio recorder or microphone but very often they will be included with the device).

For the *Digital Marketing Podcast*, we use the Zoom H4N which has two separate XLR ports, each of which can have an XLR microphone attached to it. Each XLR mic will record onto a separate channel, giving you two separate recordings to edit. As each mic has its own separate channel, the sound level of each person can be adjusted to suit the environment and voice.

We also use our Zoom H4N in the recording studio when we meet up to make recordings. It's great to ditch the laptop and have a dedicated audio capture device that's simple to use and reliably captures what we need. In the studio environment, we put in two hand-held XLR microphones to capture each of our voices. It's simple, reliable and it just works. We also end up with a back-up recording on the audio recorder's SD card. After each recording, we pull a copy of the file we have recorded onto the laptop for editing, but the master copy of the recording stays on the SD card as a go-to back-up, should we ever need it. SD card storage is so cheap you don't need to reuse the cards and delete old recordings. Just make sure you label the SD cards if you have lots of them. The only word of warning we would give you on portable recorders is... always switch them off before removing the SD card. SD cards can become corrupted if you remove them while the unit is writing files to the card.

Understanding sample rates

Many software packages or digital audio recorders will ask you for a target sample rate measured in kHz for your recording. For those of you who are curious, this is a measure of the samples per second in the recording. Don't get too hung up on it. The higher that number the clearer and more detailed the recording should be. We always stick to 44.1 kHz as this gives CD quality and is widely recommended. Avoid recording content at other sample rates and never mix different sample rate recordings in the same edit. You will know when you have done this because voices will either sound like you've been breathing helium or deep and disturbing like you just stepped out of a horror movie. If you do get this wrong it's hard to fix, so keep things consistent and get it right first time or you may find yourself re-recording your content, which is never fun.

Podcasting toolbox additions

Voice-over-IP services

Skype: https://www.skype.com

Zoom video conferencing service: https://zoom.us

Apple FaceTime: https://support.apple.com/en-gb/guide/facetime/welcome/mac

Google Hangouts: https://hangouts.google.com

Call recording software

Ecamm Call Recorder for Skype: https://www.ecamm.com/mac/callrecorder/

Audio Hijack: https://rogueamoeba.com/audiohijack/

Talkhelper: https://www.talkhelper.com

Audio editing software

Garage Band: https://www.apple.com/uk/mac/garageband/

Audacity Software: https://www.audacityteam.org

An overview of podcast editing options and how to do it

17

Editing your podcast: why edit?

There are those in podcasting who frown upon editing and take the view that you should keep it raw and real and not edit. Everyone is entitled to their opinion of course, but our guidance on this is you should edit for the sake of your audience if not for your own professional persona. Podcasting has moved on a great deal from a medium that had its origins in audio blogging. While there are some masters of 'stream of consciousness' recordings that can be hugely entertaining, we'd argue that if they pull it off, chances are they have been in the broadcasting game for a long time and know how to give a polished performance off the bat. For most of us, especially if we are just starting out, that is unlikely to be the case. Edit and edit well!

As you get more experience, you will find you need to edit less in postproduction, but when you first start, if you want to grow your audience and have a podcast that succeeds, good use of editing is going to be an essential tool in your kit. Editing skills can make or break your podcast and, if done in the wrong way, can make or break your love and passion for podcasting as a medium.

The importance of editing

Of all the skills you apply to produce a show, editing can be the most significant time-suck in terms of actual hours spent, especially when you first start out. It's easy to think you can just ramble into a directionless conversation with a guest and get away with that later by editing. The reality is, if you do this, the editing process is going to be way harder and more time-consuming than it should be. As you record more content and spend more time editing your shows together you very quickly learn that proper planning and editing walk hand in hand. The easiest and quickest episodes to edit are the ones where you have already planned out a good structure and outline of what you want to cover and how you are going to cover it before you press record. Some days when you record you will be better and more on the ball than others, but always your best episodes will typically be the ones you tackled with a nice tight plan. Focus on getting every aspect right in the original recording, so you have less work to do when editing – but always edit.

When conducting interviews with guests you never quite know what you will end up with. It's easier to cut down on editing time when working with co-hosts as you quickly get to see how each other works and thinks but when interviewing guests you won't have that luxury. Well-planned-out questions will definitely shorten your edit time but there will sometimes be angles and directions your guest speakers may take that slow down the pace of your show. Editing can solve that.

Editing time

It's important to factor in adequate time to get your editing right. It is very easy to spend three to five minutes on editing every minute of show you eventually output. If you start out with 30 minutes of recorded audio, you are typically going to have to listen to that at least three or four times to get a finished product, so don't underestimate the time you need. Like any content production process, the more raw material you start off with, the longer it will take to cut it down to size. For this reason, you might want to plan your initial show lengths accordingly. Putting out hour-long daily shows might seem like a great idea but with an hour to record and up to two or three hours to edit that's a big commitment.

A cautionary tale

When recording the *Digital Marketing Podcast*, we will often spend the first half of our day just catching up and talking about what's been going on in our space. We typically try to get together once every two months or so with the aim of recording four to eight episodes back to back. Initially, we focus on episode subject areas we want to cover, and having chosen these will map out the key areas and points we want to include. With that mapped out, we will both share and explore any additional resources we want to discuss and place these into our plan. Having worked through these, we will then record all the planned episodes back to back. The actual recording time is always a lot less than the talking, planning out and organizing part of the process. I'd say on average we spend a good two or three minutes mapping up and outlining for every one minute we record but that investment in time is well worth it. We very rarely have to spend much time editing these recordings bar removing the occasional slip-ups that result in us having to break to get the giggles they cause out of the way. That may sound like a lot of time up front, but to be honest, it's so much more fun to edit what you are going to cover together. Editing is a solo job, and it can quickly become a very dull and lonely task on an overly long recording. Do all that you can to polish your performance before you come to edit, and you will not only end up with better content, you will love the whole process a lot more.

The editing process

Everyone will naturally find a method that works for them, but to help you get started, we will share with you how we approach editing. Proper planning aside, we have found there are two stages we take when editing our podcast episodes: an initial phase we call our 'cut and shut' editing process where we organize and fine-tune the actual content we are covering in that episode, and then a secondary level of polishing individual performances. Both these stages are important, but the overall shaping and organizing of the content is by far the most crucial aspect and usually what we focus on first.

The 'cut and shut' edit

First off, when we edit a show, we will listen through the whole recording and make a few notes on what works well and what can be cut. There are a few questions you continually need to ask yourself as you listen through the content and all of them need to be asked from your audience's point of view rather than your own. What aspects of this show are boring? Do any of the sections of the recording feel slow or lacking in energy or pace? Are any elements of the content off topic from what we set out to explore and cover? What could I cut out and no one would really notice? Asking these questions will help you to identify possible edit decisions you could make to improve your finished product.

On much longer recordings we have found it sometimes helps to place splits in the audio timeline just before you ask each question and to label that section with the question. Doing this can help you to focus on what each part is trying to answer and to keep focus and pace. It also gives you a great overall view of how much time you are spending on each section of your interview to get a really great overall view of the structure and flow of it.

If elements need to be reorganized, we will do that at this stage to get a good overall shape of the episode. If our show is featuring a guest, we have found it is best to ensure the main focus is on them. It's easy when the conversation is flowing for the host to contribute more than they bargained for. When I (Ciaran) first started out interviewing I was particularly guilty of this. Taking the view that your guest star is the star is always the best policy and will help you judiciously cut back on the interviewer's contributions and opinions. It's still a balancing act of course, and sometimes these additions have to stay so that what follows makes sense, but if you can cut host interjections out and the interview still flows it is sometimes best. Occasionally when you are interviewing you know there is more your guest can say on a subject so you might throw in an additional question to tease out the content you feel they have. It's usually quite easy to cut out your teasing question and just create a longer contribution from your guest in that section of the interview. We've found that a particularly useful technique to employ if your guest is perhaps nervous or getting warmed up and into the interview process. Done well it can ensure you get to show off their skills and expertise in the best possible light.

Polishing performances

With your big edit decisions settled and the order and flow of the conversation in place, it's time for a second pass of your episode where your objective is to polish the performances of those involved. All of us will have verbal ticks that fall into our recordings. These can take the form of 'ums' and 'errs' and all sorts of involuntary noises we make while we think about what we are about to say next. Sometimes they naturally form a part of our conversation. They can also take the form of phrases repeated too frequently or overly long pauses. All too often it is only when listening back to a recording that you will notice the same involuntary noises or stock phrases or lengthy pauses occurring again and again. And it's irritating. Really irritating. If you notice them, the chances are your audience will too and it can be a real turn-off to what is actually really great content. The trick is to edit them judiciously. A few of these things left in is natural and they may run into further words; as you will learn, not all verbal ticks can be removed easily and may have to stay. However, if they are too frequent it's worth stripping out the ones you can. With time, if they are your ticks, you will learn to avoid making them in the first place, but while you get started, editing can help you to hide what you don't want heard.

Time-saving cuts

When I first started out editing, I would dogmatically cut the recording each side of the offending verbal tick, delete it and then fill the resulting gap by pulling the subsequent audio into place, so the gap created by the cut was removed. However, there is, as it happens, a quicker way which I've always called a single cut edit. If you make a cut immediately after the 'um' or 'err' you want to remove, you can just slide the audio after the cut over the offending verbal tick to remove it. With time you will quickly get to spot what many verbal ticks look like when displayed in a waveform format.

Polishing your audio content

Depending on how you captured your audio you will typically be editing either a single or multiple audio tracks. Single-track recordings are the simplest to edit. You have one audio waveform timeline in your audio editor which you can trim, cut and paste into shape. You quickly learn, though, that sometimes both people can start talking at once and there really isn't much you can do about that in a single-track recording.

Editing multiple-track recordings

A lot of the interviews we conduct are done over Skype using the Ecamm Skype recorder plugin. When you save the recording, you are given the option to save each half of the Skype conversation as separate files. This is great from an editing perspective as it gives you a lot more control during the editing process. So for example, if I am interviewing a guest in California, I will have everything they said in one audio file and everything I said in another. Both recordings will be the same length so as long as I align them in the editing software timeline when played back, they should form one seamless conversation. The only challenge with having multiple recordings is keeping them perfectly in sync. If I cut out a two-second pause on my part of the conversation, then my guest's part of the interview is going to be two seconds ahead of mine. Once that happens you are in a whole world of editing pain. So when you make a cut or a change using multiple recordings we would recommend making cut points across all your recordings at that point so they all get edited and the timing of each person's conversation stays in sync.

Voice-over-IP recording time delays

The internet is lightning fast. So lighting fast in fact that we can quickly forget the vast distances that our digital communication can take place over. For various technical reasons, long distances can result in short time delays between one person speaking and the other person receiving the information. Do what you can to smooth over and edit out these delays. Left in they can cause an interview to lose pace and feel like it's really dragging on.

Sound levels

Sound levels between different tracks sometimes need adjustment. It's easy even in a controlled recording studio environment to get different sound levels on each track. It only takes one participant to sit at a different distance to their mic, and overall volume between the tracks will be different. Some of this can be edited within your audio editing package. Most audio editing programmes will allow you to control the overall master sound level of each track as well as giving you the option to tweak sound levels within specific sections of your recording if required. There are also some post-production tools that can help fix a whole number of sound issues, which we will share with you in Chapter 21, 'Publishing and distributing your podcast'.

Top and tail your show

With your editing of the interview done, it's time to get your audio branding into place. We have a standard introduction and a wrap-up ending we call our 'intro' and our 'outro' edited up and ready to drop into our audio editing software. Actually, depending on the month we put the episode together, we usually have several outros ready to pull into place which promote different aspects of our business to our listeners. We will talk more about these elements in Chapter 21. For the moment, it's enough to say that having these pieces recorded and ready makes topping and tailing each episode a breeze.

Audio file formats

When it comes to working with your audio files there are a lot of different file formats you need to understand and get familiar with.

Uncompressed audio formats

AIFF or WAV file formats offer high-quality audio content with very little quality loss. They tend to be more commonly used for mastering your podcast shows. Using uncompressed audio formats for your original recordings will help to maintain the recording's quality. Each time you save or edit the file in your production process the quality of the recording is kept as no compression is applied. If you repeatedly save MP3 files at different stages of your production process you can begin to degrade the audio quality; stick with uncompressed AIFF or WAV formatted files and you will never hit that problem. The only downside of these formats is the files are a lot bigger than an equivalent-length MP3 file because they are not compressed. However, computer storage is so cheap these days that this really shouldn't cause you any problems. Most digital audio recorders give you the option of taking your initial recording as AIFF or WAV. We have worked with both and have had no problem with either. Our advice is pick one and stick with it for all your master recordings.

MP3

MP3 is the most commonly used file format for publishing and distributing podcasts. It offers a compact file size and is universally playable by the majority of digital devices and podcatcher apps. Because it is so universally accepted it's the best format currently available for distributing your podcasts. In addition to compressing your audio file, the file format allows you to add small amounts of additional information using a format called ID3 tags. ID3 tags are used for things like the episode title, description, author information and show artwork. We will explain a bit more about these tags and how to edit them in Chapter 21.

M4a

This format is actually a rival of the MP3 file format and can be used for publishing and distributing podcasts. Before you get confused over yet another option, let's just clear things up by saying we don't use this file format. It was created by Apple and can do some clever things that MP3s can't. As well as including a playable audio track like an MP3 does, the M4a file format allows the content producer to add chapter markers to their audio file which can include a visual image for each chapter marker. It's suited to mostly static images that can be changed at different points of the recording. When using an M4a file, users are able to skip between chapters and see different chapter artwork displayed as they do so. The overall effect is to produce something akin to a PowerPoint or SlideShare-type presentation which automatically progresses as you play the audio. If you want to have a go at playing with the chapter marker artwork feature, then Apple's GarageBand software enables you to add a visual chapter track and output in the M4a format. However, you don't have to make use of these visual chapter markers; you could just use it like an MP3 to compress and deliver your audio.

Interestingly, the format has been proven to produce a slightly smaller file size with a slightly higher sound quality than an equivalent MP3 file. Sounds brilliant, doesn't it? Well… it kind of is, but sadly the one big drawback that stops us using it is that it isn't as widely supported as the MP3 file format. It's largely going to limit your audience to those using Apple's iTunes or Apple Podcast App or on other platforms via popular video playback software. A large number of podcast platforms, MP3 players and Apps outside of Apple's ecosystem still don't support it. We have never felt that the benefits the file format outweigh the lack of universal playability, so if you do make use of it for distributing your episodes you may hit a few listener snags.

Learn to edit like a pro

Whatever audio editing software you choose it pays to get confident with how it works and what it can do to help save you time. Lynda.com features some excellent video tutorials specifically for podcasters which are regularly kept up to date with the latest versions of the software. With a couple of hours of investment, you really will get to learn your chosen tool well. Investing the time and the low monthly subscription fee for their tutorials is totally worth the effort and cost, so we have included links to some excellent audio editing software tutorials in this chapter's podcasting toolbox. If you have never used the service before you can often take advantage of a free trial, so there really is no excuse. Go check them out!

Podcasting toolbox additions

GarageBand: Online manuals are included in GarageBand. Just go to the help menu in the application.

Audacity: Check out the free online manual for Audacity: https://manual.audacityteam.org/man/tutorials.html

Tutorials to edit podcasts like a pro

Lynda.com have some brilliant video tutorials for using both GarageBand and Audacity specifically for those wanting to master podcasting editing:

GarageBand tutorial: https://www.lynda.com/GarageBand-tutorials/Welcome/495274/518588-4.html

Audacity tutorial: https://www.lynda.com/Audacity-tutorials/Welcome/518687/564759-4.html

Using interviews with influencers to maximize your podcast strategy 18

I (Ciaran) started podcasting back in 2008. At the time I was working for a non-profit sailing charity, and podcasting was a hot digital topic I was keen to explore. I'd been listening to shows for a couple of years and convinced myself it sounded pretty easy to do. In essence, it is, but as you will have gathered from this book, there is quite a steep learning curve. I'd been running my show for a few months and had quickly exhausted my initial ideas on who I could interview internally at our organization. In short, I needed new content, or the show would stutter and die. Armed with almost no interview technique and a second-hand mini-disc recorder with a microphone that I'd very proudly purchased off eBay, I proceeded to wander the Southampton Boat Show looking for possible victims to interview. I learned quite a few things that morning: firstly, that getting the interview wasn't the hard part.

In most cases, a bit of an intro on what I was doing and asking, 'Would you like to get involved?' was enough. What I hadn't bargained for was the power a microphone gives you. You see, I don't think I ended up interviewing anyone I actually approached. After my initial pitch I was immediately deferred to the most senior person on the stand. They then either presented themselves for the interview or re-heard my pitch and arranged for me to come back later to meet with their founder, CEO or nominated media spokesperson. Boy was I out of my depth! But at that stage, I had little choice but to swim hard. As soon as you have settled on a subject and a guest you had better very quickly come up with some sensible questions. Simply rocking up to an influential CEO and asking, 'So what do you want to talk about?' isn't a plan.

It sounds cringe-worthy now, but that's literally what I did. I was lucky, the CEO in question took pity on me and calmly explained that I needed to tell him that. He then actually helped me bullet point a plan, and we pulled it off. Armed with that formula my subsequent interviews went a lot better!

The other key thing I realized was that each of these people I was meeting up and interviewing were actually placing a lot of trust in me. Taking part in an interview is always something of a nervous experience for everybody. The greater steps I took to make it easy and fun for them the better we bonded. By the end of that morning at the Southampton Boat Show, I had amassed five senior contacts in companies we had never connected with before. In the space of a 15–20-minute interview, I could connect and have a shared experience with anyone in my industry and be on first-name terms with them. There really aren't many other business activities that do that. At the heart of this formula was taking a real interest in other people and what they do, and giving them something back, for free. That's always a great way to start any relationship. However, following their approval of the edited version, I found them really keen to share our joint effort with their audiences. I'd effectively stumbled on what is now called influencer marketing. It happened quite by accident, and it was only years later when looking at mainstream online influencer marketing that I realized how closely my original podcast networking formula mirrored this marketing technique.

The basics of influencer outreach

The basics of good influencer outreach are fairly straightforward. You want to take steps to identify the right influencers for your audience, and there are a couple of different strategies you can follow. We tend to focus on the content first and influence second. Pulling in the wrong guest with the wrong message could put your hard-won audience off so choose carefully. You do, however, want to keep half an eye on how each guest may be able to grow your audience. Typically, the kind of guest for audience engagement and growth will quite willingly share a link to a good interview with their own audiences either via social media platforms or through email lists they manage. Our most downloaded shows have always been shows featuring a guest who was engaged with the content and willing to share through their own channels – and this can have a significant impact on additional audience reach over time. If on top of that your content is well put together and fun, you stand a very good chance of growing your number of regular subscribers with each featured guest. Make sure you share with your guest in advance where the show will be published and provide them with an embeddable audio player and/or links so that it is super easy to share that content with their own audiences.

Spend time finding people in a particular subject area who have something valuable to contribute. For me, the message and their personality are absolutely vital. If I can, I like to be able to hear how they sound, either from other interviews they have done or at the very least a quick catch up to explore an idea over the phone well in advance of doing any actual recordings. If an interview is going to work, I have to believe that the guest I am booking is someone I can work with. I want to be confident I can make them sound good. As a podcast host, I see that as my job. It leads to a win-win. They will be proud, I will be proud, and hopefully, the audience will love it too.

Finding influencers

There are lots of useful tools that can help you identify influencers. We are big fans of the influencer marketing tools provided by Klear. They provide a great collection of free influencer tools that help you to identify, analyse and measure influencer marketing activities. Check out the link to their tools we have included in the podcast toolkit additions for this chapter.

Fine-tuning your outreach

When you first start out in podcasting, it is a lot harder to get well-known guests to appear on your show. You have yet to make a name and brand for your show, and the impact you can have for anyone famous or well-known is obviously at a minimum. As a new podcaster, of course, I know that including well-known celebrities on my show guest list will do great things for my show audience growth. However, that's a fairly one-sided value exchange for the guest you want to interview. Don't make the mistake of telling the well-known figure what appearing on your show will do for you and your show; in most cases, this won't have real value for them. What they value is what appearing on your show could do for them. Maybe it's not a topic commonly covered. Perhaps you can focus on how previous interviews have helped others you have worked with? Perhaps you can help them reach a niche audience of value to them or their business? For most well-known individuals, their time has a definite value and to access that time you need to focus on fair value exchange. We have always had a lot of success reaching out to authors of new books. They are always keen to share their knowledge and expertise and will very often provide some really great content if you provide them with an opportunity to promote their book. Keep an eye on books published that are aimed at your interest category and reach out to the authors either via social media or through the 'contact us' section of their business or book promotional websites. Read a great book on a topic that taught you lots and was well written. Why not use that as an opportunity to reach out to the author to help them promote it. Your enthusiasm and knowledge of their work will greatly aid the success of your outreach efforts.

Being your own influencer

Just as you are always after engaging guests for your podcast, there are also plenty of other podcasters out there who will be looking for guests. Appearing on someone else's show can be a great way of building your own name and brand. Every week we get an increasing number of requests from professional people keen to become a featured guest on our show. Some of these pitches shine, and others never make it past a polite reply declining the kind offer. There are a few key steps you should always take to make a good outreach pitch of your own:

1 Research the show you want to appear on and listen to a few episodes to ensure it's the right place for you to shine as a guest.

2 Write a short and to the point initial pitch email, with a couple of hot ideas on topics you would be happy covering. There are a number of templates in circulation to make writing these pitches easier, but they are so over-used they have in most cases lost their power. We get a lot of very similar-looking pitches for our show, so create something unique and very you, and stand out from the crowd.

3 Make sure you make it clear in your pitch email that you have listened to the show and highlight aspects of recent interviews or features that made their show stand out for you. Don't just try to game the system by

grabbing a few random facts; make sure you really have got to know their show before you reach out. It takes time but it will go a long way to making you more successful with your pitches.

4 Include some links to video or audio interview material that illustrates you as a voice and personality. This could be content from your own podcast or links to other interviews you have maybe given in the past. However, do ensure it isn't an interview on any of the topics you are pitching!

5 Be ready with both short (150 words) and longer-form (half- to full-page) bios that explain who you are and why you are qualified to talk on the subject you are pitching for. These bios are not used as part of the initial email pitch, but should anyone come back to you to set up an interview, it's a good idea to have these ready to send straight over, together with a couple of headshots should they want to use them.

Setting your guest at ease

When arranging an interview, I like to take time to plan out conversations in advance with the guest, so they feel they are a big part of the process and are ready for the actual interview. Some of the guests you choose to feature may be media pros and take a podcast interview in their stride, but never assume that is the case. We like to ensure that any guests are well prepped before we record. It's great to build trust by explaining the interview won't be live, so you can redo any aspects that don't go right first take. Make sure you plan in time for this. For a 15–30-minute interview, we will often ask guests to plan in double that time in their schedule to ensure there is time to get the best interview we can. Finally, we always explain to every guest that before anything is published, we will ask for their feedback and final sign-off. Again, this can go a great way to establishing trust with your guest. Many corporate employees will have to get approval from their PR or compliance team. Helping them to understand that you aren't looking to catch them out can really help to set them at ease.

Sometimes you will find a thorny issue you want to cover with a guest. You don't have to ambush a guest to include these; plan it in and work with them on it. Following this methodology means you never burn bridges and always build trust and mutual respect. That's good for business and will be great for your podcast.

Remarkably, in the eight years we have been conducting interviews we have never had any trouble securing approval from compliance teams. I think our transparency and openness to work as part of a team on the content helps to achieve this. More sensitive topics or edgier interviewing might be harder to secure approval on, but trust, if you can establish it, is a rich currency to deal in. Good interviews always come from happy, relaxed, well-prepared guests in our opinion, so we have learned to go out of our way to create the right environment for this.

Mind mapping

For planning out an interview with a guest, you can't beat a mind-mapping app. There are lots of brilliant apps and software for mind mapping, but my go-to favourite is one called Coggle.it. It's fab. It's all online, so it's easy to not only share mind maps with others but actually to work collaboratively on them. It also works really well on both desktops and smartphones.

We create mind maps for most guest episodes. In the centre of the Coggle is the main focus of the episode. Starting at 12 o'clock and moving around clockwise we will jot down the key topics we are covering, so we both have an agreed route through the show. As we and the guest talk, we will come up with questions and key interjections we or they might make. It's collaborative. Guests can add content and ideas into the plan and include any key points or figures that help them to make their point. Usually, in 10–15 minutes you can collaboratively work up an overall direction for the entire interview. It's a fantastic tool and really helps give anyone new to being interviewed an invaluable crutch to get moving with. When we or our guest make changes or additions to the Coggle document, we get alerted via email. As Coggles are stored online, we are working on the same document so we don't run into version issues or have any emailing of attachments running back and forth.

Some of the Coggles our guests have contributed to have turned out to be works of absolute genius. Guests often get inspired by the process and really map things out in beautifully clear and concise ways. Some are a bit more bare bones and just cover four to six key questions we have agreed upon, but all of them help to focus the content to an end goal in mind. It's true you could just write this kind of planning down as bullet points, but there is something about the spurs and lines of this free-flowing format that always leaves room for additional ideas.

Coggle visibility

Coggle mind maps can be public or private but basic Coggle accounts, which are free, have a limit on the number of private Coggles you can create. For obvious reasons, you should never put any sensitive information into a publicly available Coggle. Paid-for premium Coggle plans come with unlimited private Coggles for a minimal monthly or annual fee. Check out a free account and give it a try. We think you may just love it.

Podcasting toolbox additions

Klear influencer marketing tools: klear.com/free-tools

Coggle: Coggle.it

Show branding intros and outros   19

Making the right first impression

First impressions matter

The start of your show is one of the most important aspects to get right. Listeners exploring new podcasts will typically listen in to the first few seconds of a show to get a feel for what it's about and what the quality is likely going to be. In this chapter, we are going to walk you through how to wrap up and package your podcast content so that it will be found and will speak on its own for what your show represents. So sit back and let's explore your inner graphic designer and visual brand marketer as we look at the essentials you need to have in place to help your show make a good first impression and grow its audience.

Judge a book by its cover

Like all things branding related, there needs to be quality and consistency in each aspect of your podcasting product. Show titles, descriptions as well as show artwork and thumbnails, should be working together to make it clear what your show is about and help the potential user assess what they might expect from it. Taking the time to think about and learn about how to package your digital podcast product effectively is an important step to consider if you want to grow your audience quickly. All you have to do is create the right first impression.

Digital packaging: what's in a name?

It's hard to think of your lovingly crafted audio podcast as a product when you start out, but in essence that is exactly what it is. Like all products, it needs to serve or fulfil a useful purpose. Maybe that purpose is entertainment, perhaps it's inspiration, maybe it's learning and education or maybe it's all of those things? Or something completely different? The important thing to focus on is that you have identified what you are setting out to achieve for your audience and who that audience is likely to be interested in. With that set out, the marketing stage is set to create the packaging and branding for your digitally downloaded product: your podcast.

First, it's important to give your show a good title. If you browse the podcast directories in Apple or Google Podcasts, you will see they are made up of many different categories and subcategories. Exploring these to find a good place your podcast would fit into is a great first step. You will also start to notice that a lot of the titles used in most categories give an obvious sense of what the podcast is about and there is a reason for this. If we are after a podcast on a particular subject, one of the first things we will do is run a search in a podcast directory for shows on the type of information or entertainment that interests us. The results that are served up by this kind of keyword search are heavily influenced by the actual titles of the shows. Other factors like popularity and how many recent downloads or high-quality reviews can also have an effect on this ranking, but show title is definitely one of the key influencing factors. It's one of the reasons we opted for the name the *Digital Marketing Podcast*. We could just have easily settled on a name like *Marku-topia*. It's kind of cool sounding and might be the sort of thing you'd think you could develop into a brand. However, it doesn't include any of the keywords people looking for the type of content we wanted to put out would be likely to search for. Similarly, unless you are already a well-known celebrity with a following in your own particular niche or mass market, making a show with a title based upon your name probably isn't a great first move. *The Ciaran Show* would, we are sure, be a sure-fire smash hit... for the two people likely to search for it (Ciaran and possibly his mum if she could ever work out how to perform a keyword search in a podcast directory!).

When choosing a name, you also want to make sure you get one that stands out. Some of the more obvious names will, of course, have already been taken but it's important that your title and the subsequent short description do a really great job of selling to any prospective audience member what your show has to offer. Granted, if you are in a popular content space, you might have to get a little bit creative with the name. Just be sure that the artwork and the description work doubly hard for you to find the right audience for your show.

Show artwork format and sizes

In addition to your show name and description, you also need to supply show artwork. We recommend keeping this artwork standardized for your show. When you submit your show artwork in your podcast feed, it needs to fulfil many criteria. As Apple leads the way in terms of reaching audiences, we recommend following their show artwork guidelines, which conveniently can be made use of in all the other directories you might want to submit your show details to. First, it should be square in shape. Apple recommends an image sized between 1400 x 1400 pixels and 3000 x 3000 pixels. The image can be supplied in either JPEG or PNG graphics file format and the colours used need to be RGB values (Red, Green and Blue). Make sure your designer is briefed on this point as very often logo designers will work to print specifications which use CMYK colour values and, if used, these can result in some odd effects on certain devices or platforms.

You also need to consider the physical file size of your show artwork. It's recommended that it should be under 500kb in size, and depending on the format of the artwork you may find that either the PNG or JPEG format gives you a smaller file size. Your graphic designer should be able to help you with this if these technical details are making your head hurt. Just be careful not to over-compress your image as distorted or pixelated files can be rejected. If you are struggling to get your physical file sizes down, be sure to check out Squoosh, an amazing and free image compression tool from Google.

Another important thing to brief into the final design is that these images will be resized a lot as they pass between different platforms and get used for different purposes. Your show graphic could look splendid at 3000 x 3000 pixels but how well does it still read and stand out when reduced down to a 200 x 200 pixel thumbnail? Can you still read all that copy you included on the design? Remember the majority of podcasts are consumed via mobile devices so you really have to think of responsive design when designing your artwork.

Recommended show artwork summary*

- Square artwork.
- JPEG or PNG format.

- Minimum dimensions 1400 x 1400 pixels.

- Maximum dimensions 3000 x 3000 pixels.

- Resolution of the image should be 72 DPI.

- Recommended physical file storage size 500kb or less.

- Designed to work well at multiple sizes and as a thumbnail image.

*Recommended sizes 2018

So that's the physical dimension of what you need to create sorted, but what about the content inside that physical space? Well, you can learn a lot by looking at how the top shows in the Apple Podcast Directory have approached the medium of podcast cover art. Some use bright colours to help them stand out. A lot use smiling happy faces, either male or female depending on the topic and the intended audience. Typography is also used effectively to help convey the tone and character of the podcast. Make it work hard for your prospective target audience, and create something that is going to stand out in your chosen directory category.

Not great at graphic design?

Some of us are, but for the rest of us, there is Canva.com. It's a great online graphics and image editing tool which makes it super easy to create online graphics and artwork for all your online needs. If you are short on time or budget it's a great way to get started and super easy to use.

Stick to your own branding

One thing to avoid is the use of any podcast directory branding. Apple, in particular, won't allow you to use any Apple or Apple podcast logos or branding in your show artwork and Google similarly doesn't allow such practices. It might seem like the smart thing to do because you are proud of the prestigious places your podcast shows up in, but it's a sure-fire way to get your show removed from those directories.

So that's your show packaging done and sorted, right? Well, not quite. There is one final piece of the puzzle we need to complete as it's a critical part of the user journey in finding your podcast: your intro and overall audio branding within each show.

Making the right first impression

You only get one chance at first impressions, and in podcasting that could be the first 15–20 seconds of any one of your shows. Never underestimate this. It is so easy to dip into the start of any podcast within any of the podcast directories, so it's important that the beginnings of your shows make a good impression and line up with all the other audio packaging elements you will have naturally worked hard on. Just about every promotional technique you can employ will ultimately involve a potential listener and subscriber getting to one of your shows and taking an initial sneaky peek under the hood to see what it offers. If a quick dip into any of your show content doesn't cut it and fails to hold their hand and welcome them right into that episode, then you really have lost out on that opportunity. Let's take a look at a few of the elements you can use to craft an excellent first impression for your new listener's ears when they dip into your content for the first time.

Pre-intros

There are quite a few parts to the introduction of your show. Typically, most shows start with an element of pre-formatted and polished audio around 15–30 seconds in length called the pre-intro. This acts something like the audio cover of a good book. Much like the cover of a book, this audio intro is designed to provide a clear start to the episode/show and create a sense of anticipation. Some podcasts handcraft these for each episode, but we have always opted to keep the start the same. Whatever you do, keep it short and to the point. We use a very short clip of audio branding we created a few years back which we use for all of our content that includes audio. You can find this on our YouTube videos, and on any short video promos we produce. Like our visual branding it is there to set the stage and retain consistency across our digital activities.

Depending on who you are and what your show is about, these intros can include voiceovers, dramatic effects, explosions, big orchestral introductions, or not, as you see fit. The important thing is that they should set the stage of audience expectations and be consistent from show to show. For a regular audience, it's the podcasting equivalent of setting up a good story: 'Are you sitting comfortably? Good, then we shall begin.' Often people agonize over how long these should be. We think shorter is better. We use ours to welcome listeners, reinforce the name of the show and the company that produces it, Target Internet. Everything else is done in the short introduction at the start of every episode. In 10–15 seconds you can cover a lot.

You will hear a lot of podcasts including information like season and episode numbers or even date and time information. These can be useful if you are putting out regular shows with very similar content but are a bit of an overhang from how podcast listening software used to work. If your show is of a technical nature, or you are keen to encourage user feedback on particular shows, promoting and reinforcing the show episode and season numbers can be a valuable contribution. Make a call on what you really need to include and where, and once you settle on a format, stick to it. It will become an accepted part of how your show starts and audiences quickly become used to it.

Intros

For each episode, as well as your standardized intro, you will ideally need to introduce that episode. It's important for the show host or hosts to in-troduce themselves so your audience can get a feel for who is in the virtual podcasting room with them as they listen. Getting a sense of where you are and what you will be covering will also help to establish the scene, and obviously, any guests need to be introduced. With your introductions try to remember that for at least some of your listeners this will be their very first episode, so keeping introduction formats can really help to ensure no one new gets left out or is kept in the dark. You can make these sections as long as they need to be but our recommendation would be to try to get across any vital information about that episode and set expectations in the first 30 seconds to a minute if you can. If you beat around the intro-ductory bush for too long, you will lose your audience. Spontaneity is one thing, but with it, it is so easy to miss an essential aspect of a good intro-duction. We have always preferred to stick to a bit of a scripted format. If you listen to our shows you will recognize it. We welcome everybody back, introduce the show host/co-host and quickly focus the audience on what that week's episode topic will be covering. Those first few words in front of the microphone that fill the scary void of silence are always the hardest, so having a set routine helps fire us up as hosts and gets the con-versation flowing.

Episode opening and introduction might include:

- podcast name;
- episode title;
- episode number;
- music/sound effects;
- host/hosts or guest identity;
- introducing what your show is going to be about/summarizing the focus;
- any other information relevant to the show such as sponsors, recording date, event details and where the show was recorded if applicable. Not all of these elements need to be included, but it's an excellent place to make a start and to choose what's appropriate for your show and your audience. Decide how the format of your intro is going to look, create a script and largely stick to it.

Bumpers

While you are planning your audio branding it's great to include a bumper into your brief for insertable audio elements you might need for your show. A bumper is merely a short sound snippet that helps to delineate a new section or segment of your show. We don't use them a lot for our show format, but they sure are useful when you need them. We've kept ours simple, choosing to use the nine seconds of audio branding music we use at the start of the show, but you can, of course, get more elaborate if you are going to section each episode up. Custom bumpers can be created for any regular sections. Following good branding principles, it does help if each of a set of different bumpers follows a similar theme or format. That way they don't feel out of place with the overall sound theme of the show.

Outros

Outros help to signify the end of the show and wrap things up, so you don't end with a hard stop. Most shows tend to make use of them to provide any essential listener information and to house calls to action you'd like your audience to follow. You should thank the audience for listening and encourage them to perform valuable actions like submitting a review if they have enjoyed the show, or provide guidance on how to get in touch and give feedback directly to you. If you are a brand or business, you can also use the show outro to highlight services or features of your product or service that your audience might want to take an interest in. We have always made use of our show outro to encourage listeners to leave reviews in iTunes as this is a great way to help boost the overall performance of your show.

Inviting feedback and user input

In the early days of podcasting, podcasters used simple voicemail services to gather audio feedback or input from users, but this has evolved. Take a look at SpeakPipe.com. SpeakPipe is a hugely popular option for gathering audio feedback from podcast listeners because it makes the whole process so simple. Once set up, the SpeakPipe widget can be embedded into any web page and will allow your listeners to leave messages for you. Depending on the subscription level to the service you choose, the audio feedback can be anything from three to more than 10 minutes. Once recorded, the messages are stored on SpeakPipe's server and can be downloaded in MP3 format.

Listener feedback

Gathering listener feedback via an audio voicemail tool can not only be a great way of hearing back from your listeners, but it can also be feedback or questions you use on your shows to generate further content. It's not right for every type of show, but it's definitely something you should consider. Engaging with audience members like this can really help to create a feeling of audience involvement and community. If you can engage more listeners in this way it is also far more likely that these featured listeners will help spread the word about your show, as they have effectively become a part of it. Don't be afraid to try something like this out for fear you might get swamped with responses. In our experience, it takes time for listeners to reach out and make contact with you and most listeners are just happy to continue quietly listening to the quality content you will be producing for them. Once you start to get feedback and feature it, you will see more listeners stepping up to the mark and taking the plunge to get involved, but it's usually a slow burn before that happens. Give it a go if it feels like a good fit for your show and stick with it for a while to give your audience a chance to warm up to the idea.

Podcasting toolbox additions

Apple Podcast Directory: To get to this you need to download iTunes and look for podcasts in the iTunes Store: https://www.apple.com/uk/itunes/

Canva: graphic design tool: https://www.canva.com/

SpeakPipe voice messaging service: https://www.speakpipe.com/

Squoosh.app: An amazingly powerful and free image compression tool: https://squoosh.app

Podcast advertising and monetization

20

Where to begin and how to manage

Inspiration for monetization

In this chapter, we are going to explore some of the options you can choose with advertising as well as some of the potential downsides to each of these options. If you read some of the hype around highly successful podcasts, you might be forgiven for believing that podcasting is the easy route to great riches. Don't believe the hype. While it is possible to generate revenue from any podcast, the majority of podcasters will do so by combining a variety of different revenue sources. In this chapter we take a look at all of the sources of revenue podcasters can take advantage of to monetize their podcasting activities.

Podcast monetization case studies

It's always great to see how other successful podcasters are monetizing their podcasts so in this chapter we have picked out a few podcasts effectively practising some of the techniques we are outlining, so you can see the methods in practice. Take a look at how these podcasts have opted to do it and maybe treat yourself to some podcast swag and Patreon bonus content while you are at it.

Understanding podcasting advertising mechanics

Most digital mediums stream their content directly from the servers that are storing the content to the end user. This streamed content is experienced the moment it is requested. When content is streamed, detailed measurement about the content being consumed is possible via website analytics and greatly helps both content producers and advertisers to understand how much content was consumed, when and by whom. Even better, because it's all being delivered on request, additional dynamic content such as advertisements can be inserted into the material and tailored to the consumer's known interests at that moment. It is this visibility and measurement of online content that has made it so popular with advertisers, driving continually increasing advertising spends year after year.

Podcasting as a format doesn't have this level of visibility or targeting for advertisers. Podcasting generally isn't served up as it's consumed like most other digital content online. Compressed audio files like the MP3 format commonly used for podcasting are fantastic for delivering high-quality audio content in relatively small files. However, these audio formats don't support sending information back to content providers on what was listened to or when different files were consumed offline or by whom. So, as a podcast producer you are limited to looking at how many MP3 files were downloaded from your hosting server for each episode you produce and getting a rough sense of the geography of the devices requesting those files for each episode. We will explore what you can measure in more detail in Chapter 22, but for now, just clock that targeting specific demographics or user behaviour, like you can on your website or via social platforms like Facebook or YouTube, isn't possible for podcasts. This lack of an ability to target specific users in the same way as you can with other digital formats makes podcast advertising a harder sell for content creators. You can raise revenue from your audience, but as we shall see, audience numbers need to be very large before advertising revenue becomes significant.

Advertising formats

There are two broad categories of advertising commonly employed on podcasts that are worth exploring in more detail: native and non-native ads.

Native ads

The native ad format is one of the most popular categories of podcast advertising. IAB research in 2017 showed that host-read native ads continue to be the preferred ad type, representing more than two-thirds of ad types in 2017 (IAB, 2017).

The term native advertising comes from the fact that ad content and its format are seamlessly woven into the show's content. Native adverts can provide fun, interesting or entertaining content via the host if done well. The trick is to find relevant advertising partners for your show so you can integrate their ad slots into the show, so they feel a natural part of it. If the ad slot is all a part of the fun and flow of the show, then it will more likely engage the listener, so they are less likely to skip. Direct response advertisers looking to drive attention on a specific offer or deal love the native ad format because it enables them to leverage on the trust the host has built with the show's audience. Some have seen results two or three times more effective than from native ad campaigns.

The downside of native ads

The one downside of native ads is actually also a strength. To do them well takes a lot of effort. You have to find the right advertisers for your audience, or the relationship is never going to last long. Remember advertisers don't spend money on advertising for the benevolent aim of financing your podcasting dreams. They want hard and fast results. You need a good fit between the interests of your audience and the needs of your advertiser and that won't necessarily come from taking the first advertisement offer that comes along. Native ads done well also take time to deliver. Don't make the mistake of badly reading the ad slot out dogmatically with the apparent sound of paper shuffling that can often occur when it's hurriedly slipped in. Work hard to make it blend in as a natural part of the show.

Non-native ads

Non-native ads are so-called because the format of the actual advert is clearly not a part of the original production. Very often they will take the form of a pre-recorded advert supplied by the advertiser for insertion into the podcast. These ads can be inserted manually by you as part of the editing process or dynamically by an ad network you have hooked up with. There are usually a few different spots you can sell to advertisers. Pre-roll ad units can be sold which play before the podcast episode starts, and mid-roll ad spots will play within the show content, often between show segments or where you place the insertion points for your ad network to dynamically insert the content. You can also sell post-roll spots where the ad content is played at the end of the episode.

The downside of non-native ads

If you have ever listened to podcasts using non-native ad spots you will be well aware of the flaw in this advertising model. We all do the same thing. As soon as we hear a different voice and an easily recognizable radio ad style, we skip forward 15–30 seconds. The ability to do this is actually one of the strong points of the podcast format from the listener's point of view. From an advertiser's perspective, this behaviour is bad news. As podcast content is mostly downloaded and played offline, it's hard for advertisers to get a measure on how many ads are being skipped. If our own behaviour is anything to go by we know, deep in our hearts, that it is a high number. This truth is one of the significant factors that keep non-native ad CPM (cost per mille, or 1,000 ad impressions) rates painfully low.

Advertising networks

There are a growing number of advertising networks that have been set up to help match podcasters with potential advertisers keen to reach podcast audiences. Marketers have increasingly begun to realize that podcast audiences are super engaged with the shows they regularly listen to. There is also a lot of research that suggests that podcasting reaches certain parts of the younger demographic that are hard to reach via traditional mainstream advertising sources such as TV and print media. A study by the IAB predicted that US podcast advertising revenue alone was expected to grow more than 110 per cent by 2020, to $659 million (IAB, 2017).

Dynamic insertion

Some advertising networks offer podcasters the ability to have adverts dynamically inserted into their shows. As an advertiser you can sign up to the advertising network and provide the required insertion points for ads and the ad network will recruit the advertisers and ad recordings to place into your show and deliver on an agreed CPM based on the total number of downloads the show generates. While the content will typically be non-native, for the advertiser there are some benefits to this kind of insertion. Past episodes of popular shows can continue to see large downloads way past the original publishing time. With dynamic insertion, adverts can be adjusted over time to ensure they are always current and in the moment.

Dynamic insertion is not just limited to pre-recorded radio-style ads either. Some shows will offer native dynamically inserted ads, working with the advertiser to handcraft a read spot by the host or even a full host endorsement of the product, which is dynamically added into shows at a fixed CPM with a targeted audience reach. In such instances, the ad will run until the purchased number of dynamic insertions has been reached. As you might imagine, this type of native dynamic insertion is a lot of extra work for podcast producers. The majority of dynamically inserted ads are still non-native, but we mention it because it offers an exciting opportunity for both podcasters and advertisers to collaborate more effectively.

Podcast advertising revenue models

Raising advertising revenue from podcasting is a challenge. Most advertising for podcasts is sold on a CPM basis. Rates per 1,000 impressions vary depending on the subject of your content and the type of audience it might pull in, but in the region of $18–$25 per 1,000 ad impressions is fairly typical. Before most brands would consider advertising or sponsoring your content, you will need to have grown a large enough and engaged enough audience to make it worth the advertisers' spend. Many advertising networks supply podcasters with the option to sell space to potential advertisers. However, some of these won't even consider signing you up for their network until you can command regular episode audiences of between 5,000 and 10,000 listeners. Until you reach that point, you are unlikely to look particularly attractive to mainstream advertisers with the big budgets to make you profitable. You also need to bear in mind that a lot of these networks and their advertisers focus on US audience exposure so you could find your audience figures aren't as attractive to them if you don't hit the magic number of listeners in that territory. That may seem harsh and disheartening, but you have to be realistic and to understand that your show is just one of the thousands of opportunities marketers have for driving awareness about their own products digitally.

How much money can you make?

The amount you can charge for adverts depends on many things. Advertisers may choose to look at many different factors including the size and reach of your audience, audience demographics, the category/content of your show, publishing frequency, social media following and much more. Many of the advertising networks cite that on average, podcasts are seeing $18–$20 CPM for 30-second spots and up to $25 CPM for 60-second spots. If you run the maths on those figures, then for a 30-second spot to an audience of 10,000 listeners you could make gross advertising revenue of between $180–$200, but you have to subtract your ad network fees from this, which can be as high as 30 per cent, giving you $126–$140.

Do you want advertising in your show?

You also need to question whether you even want to allow advertisements into your show. Many people love podcasting because it is different from commercial radio and isn't filled with inserted ads that interrupt their enjoyment of the programme with audio designed to assault the listener's ears. The more you fill your podcast with interruptive ads, the more you will potentially slow the growth of your audience. The decision on how to monetize and how you want to do that needs careful consideration and shouldn't be rushed into.

If you are a brand and are starting a podcast to engage with your core customers and drive a deeper level of engagement from important and valuable segments of your customer base, then why would you even consider cheapening your content by allowing others to hijack your audience's attention with paid-for advertising and sponsorship? We would argue that doing so could devalue what you are offering and water down the overall brand-building effect it could have for you.

So that's the downside of advertising. Don't let that put you off. We just want to help manage your expectations a little in advance of any initial disappointment you might feel when you first dive in. It's certainly not the only way to monetize your content.

Show merchandise

If you have a show with a loyal following, promotional items could offer a great way to monetize your show. Books, t-shirts, sweatshirts, mugs, pens, tote bags, drinks coasters, the list of potential podcast-related swag and merchandise is almost endless. There are two choices when going down the merchandising route. It is possible to buy, sell and dispatch your show merchandise manually. Doing it all yourself will help to drive income.

However, you can quickly become consumed with managing the ordering, production, fulfilment and customer service surrounding the products you have on offer. Fortunately, in our marvellous digital age, there is another option for the busy podcaster focused on their audience and show content.

Print on demand/drop-shipping

For most podcasters, outsourcing all of the work around providing show merchandise is the sensible option to take. If you would like someone else to take care of selling merchandise, managing stock levels and delivering your orders then the print-on-demand/drop-shipping route is the way to go. All you have to do is to supply the designs, and a good drop-shipping partner will do the rest for you. The profit you make on each product sold will typically be a lot less but it's a much more frictionless business model for the busy podcaster. There are lots of these services available worldwide; which one you choose will largely depend on what merchandise you want produced and where you will need the service to deliver the products. As you can imagine, the options for service providers in the print-on-demand market are vast and changing all the time. If you want to learn more about the print-on-demand/drop-shipping world, we recommend *Merch and the World of Print on Demand* (Topping, 2018). It's packed full of over 35 different print-on-demand services and includes really hands-on advice for setting up your shop on multiple platforms and how to automate and streamline your product services.

CASE STUDY   My Dad Wrote A Porno

Show website: www.mydadwroteaporno.com
Store: www.mydadwroteaporno.com/merch-new

A global hit, this comedy podcast has grown a loyal fan base across the world and it's hardly surprising. It's not everyone's cup of tea we are sure, but we have yet to find anyone who has listened who doesn't quickly become addicted to this humorous exploration of one of the host's father's attempts to outdo the publishing sensation that was *50 Shades of Grey*. The team behind the podcast offer an extensive range of podcast merchandise, and we think it's a great example of how widely available products like t-shirts, mugs and tote bags can be transformed into must-have items any fan would be proud to own.

Sponsorship

Invite your listeners to be your sponsors

Patreon is a membership service that provides business tools for content producers to run a subscription content service. It's a great platform for helping you to connect with your users and receive regular subscriptions or donations from them. They also allow content providers to further build relationships with their patrons by providing exclusive experiences for their subscribers through the Patreon service. Started back in 2012, the platform supports over 100,000 creators, charging just 5 per cent on any donations made to fund the service, plus a further 5 per cent to cover transaction fees. Many podcasters are able to generate a healthy contribution to their running costs, and a few have actually been in a position to quit their jobs entirely with the revenue and support created. Check out the service at www.patreon.com

CASE STUDY   Ologies

Show website: www.alieward.com/ologies/
Show merchandise: ologiesmerch.com
Show Patreon page: www.patreon.com/ologies

Hosted by writer, science correspondent and TV host Alie Ward, *Ologies* is an excellent example of where following your passions can take podcast content. Ward interviews experts she meets from a vast range of science-related disciplines. From aerology to zymology, Ward interviews the unsung heroes of the lab coat world in an entertaining and absorbing way. A passion project, Ward didn't want her show 'getting gummed up with obnoxious advertising', as she explains in the video introduction to her Patreon page (Ward, 2018). She has taken a non-advertising approach to monetization. As well as the merchandise store, the show also has its own Patreon page with tiered offerings starting at $1 per show, which enables Patreons to submit questions to the featured 'Ologists' before shows are recorded. Five levels of Patreon support are available, ranging from $1 to $25 a month. The more help you give the show financially, the more benefits you unlock as a Patreon. Definitely subscribe to this podcast if you enjoy expanding your knowledge in a highly entertaining way, but also take a look at the *Ologies* Patreon page and be inspired by what you could support and create for your show.

Sponsors

Finding sponsors is a great way to monetize your podcast if you can find the right fit for your audience and content. Sponsorships can be offered on a one-off episode basis, or they can be sold to the same advertisers for multiple episodes and increased exposure for that advertiser to your audience. Carefully crafted sponsorship deals offer a much stronger relationship between the advertiser, the podcast producer and the audience. When selling sponsorship of your show, you really can push the boat out to ensure the maximum exposure for sponsors in really smart and creative ways. Just be aware that such careful crafting takes time and commitment to get working. However, because you can custom fit a sponsor's needs around the interests of your listeners and offer something more bespoke and unique, sponsorship can command much higher levels of revenue than plain ads do. How much revenue you can command will be closely tied to the ability to negotiate with each sponsor based on your content focus, audience size and location.

Finding the right sponsors

This doesn't need to get complicated. Sometimes advertising networks can help put you in touch with suitable sponsors but remember they will want to take their cut of any revenue for doing so. Plan out brands who may want to sponsor your content and approach them. As we mentioned, to be attractive you need to have gained a reasonably sized audience or be serving a smaller, harder-to-reach niche audience that advertisers might highly value. Think about brands or services that might be appealing to your audience and reach out personally to those brands. The key to these approaches is to think about what your audience might be able to do for the organizations you reach out to and focus on those benefits. Any deals will need to be negotiated. Reach out and establish whether there is interest first before putting the proposal together. If you have a personal contact who can introduce you to someone at that organization, that is always a good place to start. Don't launch in straight away with a pitch to the first name you get; ask your contact who the best person to approach would be, and take things from there.

CASE STUDY   Lore

Show website: https://www.lorepodcast.com
Show merchandise: http://theworldoflore.com
Show Patreon page: https://www.patreon.com/lorepodcast

Aaron Mahnke's *Lore* podcast was an instant hit with listeners, quickly growing large audiences who became addicted to the show's fortnightly true-life scary stories. The format includes Mahnke reading these stories set against specially written music that creates the perfect atmosphere for engaging oral storytelling. If horror, fiction or storytelling are your thing you have to listen to this podcast; it will most certainly inspire you.

Merchandise

The show's producer releases books of the stories covered in the podcast on a regular basis for listeners to purchase. They have also teamed up with drop-ship company CottonBureau.com, who deal with all the hard work behind selling, printing, shipping and customer service for the show's other merchandise.

Sponsors

Lore provides a great example of how to integrate sponsor-related content into episodes without interfering with the show's content. Sponsors are given exposure within that episode's show notes by the producer. Sponsored episodes also include a dedicated section where the sponsors are given some airplay, and any offers being provided to listeners are explained. These are read out by the show's host, Aaron Mahnke and fit in well to the overall show. The sponsor sections are positioned so that there is additional must-hear content related to that episode's story following the sponsor's slot. This is so much better than merely tacking the sponsor section onto the start or end of a show as it strategically increases the chance the sponsor's message will be listened to. The show notes are also published alongside that episode within the show's podcast website, with sponsors' details clearly visible.

Each sponsor is also advised to create a custom landing page specifically for their sponsored offering, which is usually the sponsor's website address with '/Lore' tagged onto the end. Working with dedicated podcast-specific landing pages is a great way to structure the offers as it gives advertisers a great measure of how many website visits and offer conversions each sponsorship slot has driven. We also liked the consistency of always using '/Lore' as the landing page address as it's super easy for listeners to follow and remember. By structuring the podcast sponsorship message in this way, the results driven from the advertising are really transparent for the advertisers.

Check it out and see how they've done this; it's a great example of a 'win, win, win' format for advertiser, producer and audience.

Patreon

Like *Ologies*, *Lore* has a Patreon page, with multiple tiers of patronage available to fans of the show. They also offer Patreon member-only episodes which are promoted in their free standard episodes. This is a great way of highlighting the benefits of Patreon membership for your show. If you have just enjoyed that week's great new episode, why wouldn't you want to sign up for a small monthly feed to get more? It's a simple but very effective way to grow your show's financial support.

Podcasting toolbox additions

Patreon: http://www.patreon.com

Ad network examples

Looking for advertising networks to size up and check out? There are lots you can choose from, but here are a few you can explore and find out more about:

Midroll: www.midroll.com/podcasters/

AdvertiseCast: www.advertisecast.com/monetize-your-podcast

PodGrid: podgrid.com

Archer Avenue: archeravenue.com

Authentic Shows: authenticshows.com

A winning formula and a caution!

Ad networks all have their own business terms of service and conditions. As with all binding business contracts, it's essential you check the small print before you sign up. Make double sure you look at what you are agreeing to before you jump into any ad network agreement or you may end up giving up more control of your content than you had bargained for. Try to aim for a triple-win scenario: a win for you, a win for your listeners and a win for your advertisers. Achieving that is a delicate balancing act, and requires a lot of attention to detail, planning and forethought. Don't rush it.

References and further reading

IAB

IAB (2017) Full year 2017 podcast ad revenue study [online] www.iab.com/wp-content/uploads/2018/06/2018_IAB_Podcast_Ad_Rev_Study_vFinal.pdf [last accessed 04 November 2018]

Print on demand/drop-shipping

Topping, J (2018) *Merch and the World of Print on Demand* (Gumroad e-book) [online] gumroad.com/l/LzoyC [last accessed 04 November 2018]

Non-advertising approach to monetization

Ward, A (2018) Patreon overview video [online] www.patreon.com/ologies/overview [last accessed 04 November 2018]

Publishing and distributing your podcast

21

To publish and distribute a podcast you basically need three things: an episode in the correct audio format you wish to publish, a website to act as a home for your show, and an RSS feed to make broadcasting out to the whole world possible. In this chapter we are going to work through each of these things, so you understand what they all are and how they work together to get your content out to the world.

Getting your podcast episode ready to publish

So at this stage, we are going to assume you have followed all our advice in the preceding chapters and have your first show edited and almost ready to publish. We say almost because before you publish you need to ensure the file you put out is compressed and in a suitable format to be played on the majority of podcast audio players. For maximum playability that means creating an MP3 file. Uncompressed audio files are huge and are not ideal for online distribution; they simply take way too long to download and take up way too much space once you have them. MP3 is an excellent online audio file format because it offers good file size compression and is still able to retain high levels of sound quality. Other file formats are available, as we discussed in Chapter 17, but none of them are as universally accepted as the MP3.

Understanding audio file compression

When you compress audio files, you get to choose how much compression is applied to the file. The more you compress, the smaller the file size, but to get really small file sizes you have to sacrifice some of the audio quality. The amount of compression is usually expressed in kbps, which stands for kilobytes per second. Most software gives you a choice of bitrate values; commonly used bitrates for compression include 95 kbps, 128 kbps, 192 kbps and 256 kbps. The higher the number, the less the file is being compressed and the better the overall audio quality will be, but the larger your finished episode will be in terms of megabytes.

So which bitrate should you choose? Well, for most spoken word recordings the most commonly recommended bitrate for MP3s is 96 kbps. If your show includes stereo music as part of your intro or outro, then you should probably opt for 128 kbps. If you are crafting a high-fidelity audio experience for your users and want to appeal to real audiophiles, then opting for a higher rate of 256 kbps might be the right solution. Some compression software includes the option for a variable bitrate; avoid this option, as it can cause playback issues in some players.

Mobile and broadband speeds are getting faster, so the physical media file size is less of an issue for users than it used to be. Our advice is to pick one that works for your show and stick to it.

Mastering file compression and audio quality

Audio quality and output formats can be a little bewildering to anyone new to the podcast space but fear not: we've got a secret weapon for sound and audio quality we want to share with you. This isn't a substitute for doing everything you can to get things into good shape when you actually record, but it is a brilliant time saver and overall magic solution not only for getting your file in the right format but also for mastering your sound levels within that recording. In our opinion, it could save you hundreds of hours over the course of your podcasting year!

The tool is called Auphonic, and you can try it out for free. Just sign up for an account, which comes with enough credit each month to work Auphonic's magic on up to two hours of audio. If you want more than two hours, you can purchase additional credits. To use the service simply export your edited show in a high-quality format such as ACC or WAV and upload that file into Auphonic for processing. The system will analyse your audio levels in the uploaded master file and output an edited version with your sound levels expertly adjusted by their audio algorithm. It can also help to clean up background noise issues.

The file you output for Auphonic can be set to compile in multiple audio formats, including the all-important MP3. If you have opted to edit your audio files in Audacity, having the option to convert the WAV files that Audacity outputs is a bonus, as Audacity doesn't support MP3 file export out of the box.

Auphonic's online interface allows you to set up some useful attributes to the finished output file, including show title, and description details as well as show artwork and publishing data. You can also control the file's loudness measured in LUFS.

LUFS

LUFS is a measurement scale used to help broadcasters keep the perceived volume of the different shows and adverts the same, and it stands for Loudness Units Relative to Full Scale. It is sometimes called LKFS, but they're actually exactly the same thing. Sounds overly technical doesn't it? Don't be intimidated though. The idea behind it was that if the loudness of all recordings could be standardized to a set level, then it would stop consumers from constantly reaching for their volume controls on different devices. It's actually a really great idea. The problem is, different organizations in the broadcast industry are all pitching for slightly different levels of standardized loudness. The music and broadcast industries have primarily adopted the LUFS level of −16, but for many online content providers including Spotify, YouTube and Amazon Alexa, the currently recommended standard loudness level is −14 LUFS, which is slightly louder than the broadcast standard. What do all these minus numbers mean? Essentially, the lower the minus number, the louder the standardized audio will be. For podcasters, setting the LUFS level of your audio files isn't a feature readily available in a lot of the audio editing packages, but Auphonic comes to the rescue with an option to set the loudness levels for your show. We've settled on −14 LUFS as our current standard loudness level as we find it works pretty well in a variety of situations and it's preferred by Spotify and audio assistant devices like Amazon's Alexa. We take the view that users can always turn things down, but it's hard to add additional volume if it isn't there. Where you set your own show's LUFS level is up to you, just remember that the broadcast industry standard is currently −16 LUFS.

So at this stage, we have our file compressed as an MP3 and ready to inject into our RSS feed so that it can be globally enjoyed by our rapidly growing and enthusiastic army of loyal podcast listeners. Let's explore how that MP3 magically gets distributed around the world using the power of your RSS feed.

Understanding RSS feeds

The term 'RSS feed' might sound complicated but it's really not. It's just a small text file that contains details of each episode together with the online location of any associated files such as your show artwork and the audio file of the actual episode. This small file is stored on a web server so that its address can be shared with multiple services that serve up and index podcasts. It is actually the same technology that powers a lot of news and blog content distribution. The only difference is that a podcast RSS feed doesn't just contain links to text-based articles and images; it serves up a whole bunch of other stuff that is all podcast-related so that the audio of your show is accessible as well. The great thing about RSS is that it is a universally standardized format, so every service or app that reads RSS does so largely in the same way. There are a few services that have their own specific tags and information as we shall discuss, but by and large it's all standardized so your content in the feed can be universally read and distributed globally without any hiccups.

As a podcaster, you can submit your RSS feed to services like Apple Podcasts, Google Podcasts, Spotify, Stitcher and numerous other podcast directories for free. Armed with this data they can index your show and provide it for their users to subscribe to and download. Individual podcast apps can also make use of your RSS feed address to subscribe their users with your content. It all starts with and relies on your updated RSS feed file. Think of it like a mini-index of all your show content. Every time you update the feed with details of a new episode, every app or podcast directory that has your RSS feed address will automatically be updated with details of your new content. Should users of these apps or services want to download that content, the RSS feed can automatically deliver them all the files they need because it knows where they are all stored. It's simple but brilliant, and it's what makes podcast publishing possible.

You could create an RSS feed using a text editor if you understand the RSS 2.0 file format. However, most podcasters are way too busy to hand-code their RSS feeds and to be honest there are a lot of different tools and services that will do this for you, so you don't have to worry about all that RSS technical stuff.

Storing your podcast for distribution

For your RSS feed to work, you are going to need some web server space to upload your audio files to. Once your show files have been given a permanent home on the web, they can have a permanent and globally accessible web address that can be included in your RSS feed so everyone can download them. You could just upload your audio files to any website space you have read-write access to. However, most website server space isn't designed for this purpose. Most website hosting packages come with something called a bandwidth limit and exceeding that limit can be an expensive thing to do.

What is bandwidth?

In website hosting terms, bandwidth is merely a measure of how much data is transferred from a website to its users. Most website hosting packages will charge a flat fee and set a limit on the total amount of data a site can use; if you exceed this bandwidth limit, you can be charged on top of your monthly fee.

Audio files are large in size compared to image and text files that make up the majority of websites. A half-hour show might be 25–39 MB in size. If you make that file available to the hundreds or thousands of subscribers you will very quickly exceed the bandwidth limits that come with most website hosting packages. Factor in multiple episodes of this size which you will produce over time and you can see how the amount of bandwidth your website consumes can rapidly escalate to hundreds of gigabytes. That could translate to some very unexpected bills vastly more than your standard monthly website hosting fee. So what is needed is a dedicated podcast hosting service for your audio files. Armed with that, you will be able to actually enjoy the success and growth of your show rather than live in fear of the additional bandwidth charges it might incur.

Adding show meta information to ID3 tags

As well as including your episode's audio, MP3 files have the ability to store some useful information about each show, including its full title, a short description of the show and useful publishing details like episode and season numbers, copyright details, artist and publisher names, and even show artwork. These useful snippets of information are stored in a format called an ID3 tag, and it's a format unique to MP3 files. It's actually one of the features that set MP3s apart; many common audio formats like WAV simply don't support the storing of text details and artwork. Much of the information stored in your ID3 tags will also be supplied in your RSS feed, but it's great to have these details physically embedded into the audio file, since many podcast player apps will make use of them so that the file can be indexed, stored and enjoyed by users. If you are using Libsyn to host your podcast, then their publishing process can take care of placing your ID3 tags into the finished published MP3. However, there is something quite satisfying about being able to master and control what goes where in your polished masterpiece's ID3 tags, so we are going to share with you a couple of ways you can sort them.

Edit your ID3 tags with iTunes

Apple's iTunes software is actually a very capable ID3 tag editor. Simply drag your MP3 file into the iTunes interface, right click or control click and select 'get info' from the pop-up menu. You can now add or edit the ID3 tags using this interface, including adding artwork. Just be sure to add a JPEG file sized between 1400 x 1400 pixels and 3000 x 3000 pixels and with a physical file size of less than 500 kb. We used this interface for years when compiling the *Digital Marketing Podcast* and it never let us down. Once you have finished, simply close the 'get info' interface and drag or export the file from iTunes to a folder on your computer ready to upload to your podcast hosting service.

Grammarly to the rescue

Grammarly is an online grammar and spell-checking solution. It's not strictly speaking a podcasting tool at all, but we have found it invaluable as a part of our podcasting publishing process. It's very easy when you edit together and publish our content to develop a complete blindness to any spelling or grammatical errors that creep into your copy as you work through publishing your episodes. Grammarly provides a browser extension for Chrome and Safari, so everything you type online can be proofed for spelling and grammar. The free version is very good, and their premium version is even better – it will help not only to catch errors but to refine and improve your writing.

Keyword stuffing and how to avoid it

For many years some podcasters have exploited how podcast search functionality keys into the words or phrases featured in key show text such as the episode title, episode description and author tags. They stuff keywords into their titles' descriptions and author tags to game the system and have their shows come up more often in user searches. Don't follow this practice. Apple, in particular, have been coming down hard on podcasters who are misusing the title and author tags to game their search results.

Best practice is that your titles and descriptions should read well and make sense to your average user. When filling out your show titles, even more care is required. Use punctuation sparingly and don't write titles all in block capitals. Also, avoid using unusual characters or text emojis to try to stand out: it's a spammy practice and is frowned upon. Use your author tag, to include the name of the host and guest/guests and not much more. Play it safe with your episode tags and keep your titles, descriptions and author tags clean, simple and to the point. By all means make use of more obvious subject keywords in your subject titles but don't repeat them unnecessarily or cram in additional words to help get your content found. It may well have the exact opposite effect.

Distributing to multiple destinations

Distributing your podcast is a relatively straightforward thing to do. Once you have uploaded the content to your hosting server and your RSS feed has updated, all the locations that have your RSS feed will have access to the new episode and start to distribute it to subscribers and make the new episode available through their directories. The focus of the podcaster should be on making sure that all the key podcast distribution services have access to the RSS feed address. Apple's Podcast Connect is going to be your main distribution channel and we will cover how to get set up there in the next chapter, but there are a number of other networks you can make sure are aware of your show. iTunes, Spotify, Google Podcasts, and Stitcher are all key locations to ensure your podcast is being distributed to, so in this section we are going to walk you through each of these and explain how you go about getting listed. All you need to start submitting your podcast is your RSS feed address and some time to work through each destination and its specific requirements. If you are hosting through a dedicated podcast hosting provider be sure to check out their documentation and how they can help with getting destinations set up as they can often streamline the process for you.

Spotify

Many of the dedicated podcast hosting companies have made it super simple to register your podcast on Spotify: just fill out the forms provided and wait to hear back. However, if they don't offer this service you can use the Spotify for Podcasters submission service at podcasters.spotify.com. It's an easy process and you can be up and running in Spotify in a matter of hours. Spotify requires you to have at least one episode in your show that is being served out by your RSS feed. Once your podcast is within Spotify, they provide you with reports on how your shows are performing within the Spotify for Podcasters service. If you submitted your show through your podcast hosting service, then they will usually provide you with these Spotify usage stats within your hosting account.

iTunes Podcast Connect

Before you can start reaching the vast audiences for your podcast in iTunes and Apple Podcasts, you will need to register for the Podcast Connect service. Doing so is easy. Visit their website and sign in with an Apple account. If you have any IOS or Mac devices, you will most likely already have one of these you can use, but if you are setting up a podcast for business or for a friend it's a good idea to set up a new account specifically to manage the podcasts. That way, should you ever part company the Podcast Connect account can just be handed over.

Once you have your Podcast Connect account, you can submit your podcast to Apple Podcasts. To do this, you will need to fill out a few details about your podcast, select a suitable category for it and provide an active RSS feed with at least one published episode in it. Getting accepted for Apple's podcasting directories isn't an instant process, and we think it's a good idea to get listed and ready with a Podcast Connect account before you start publishing for real. Doing this is relatively easy: create an episode zero!

Episode zero

Think of episode zero as a short promo that highlights what your show is all about. It acts as a great way to build up the expectation about your show and once launched it's the perfect place that anyone new to your podcast can turn for that all-important initial pitch and experience of content from you. If you have some of your up-and-coming content recorded you could include short clips to give a flavour of what you will be offering. Mix this together with an audio introduction to you and any co-hosts, and you have the perfect vehicle to tease people into your show. By all means get creative but keep it short and snappy and to the point. Far better to leave people wanting more with a quick promotion than to bore them into submission with 15–20 minutes of what you aren't quite doing in full yet! You can mark this episode up as number zero when you submit it to any of the key podcast destinations you have set up to distribute out to. Most of these services require you to have a fully functioning RSS feed with at least one episode in it; an episode zero will fulfil that requirement so you can start getting your show seeded to all the different locations you will want to push out to. When you do release your first full episode you will be up and running everywhere you want to be: no waiting to be accepted for different locations.

Even if you already have an established podcast, creating an episode zero is a great idea. It allows you to put together a short promotional show that explains who you are and what your podcast is going to be about. Don't feel that once it's created you can't update it at a later date: you absolutely can and should. Episode zeroes are very often where new listeners will ear-test your show, so keep it current.

Content ratings

Apple also asks you to rate your content either clean or explicit. This rating helps them to ensure that the right content is made available to the right audiences. This is important not only for parental controls but also because some countries do not permit explicit content. Incorrectly labelling your content as clean when it includes explicit elements can result in your episode or show being removed from Apple's directories so always fill this out correctly. If you want to truly reach the maximum international audience, avoid any bad language or obscenity in your shows. You only need one episode to include such content, and you can find your show being removed from countries where such material isn't allowed. In essence, keep your show content clean, edit out any profanity, and you gain access to potentially millions of more ears around the world.

Google Podcasts

Google recently updated their main podcast destination. For a long time, podcasts were distributed through Google Play, but in 2018 that all changed and they now offer a dedicated podcast distribution network called Google Podcasts. If you are hosting your show's web pages with your podcast hosting service, they should have everything set up so your show website is ready for Google Podcasts. It you have opted to host show pages on your own web space and want to get your show listed in Google Podcasts, you will need to add some code to your show web pages. Now, this does get a bit technical if website coding isn't your thing but don't let that put you off. Google has documented the process in detail so you can pass the link we have included in this chapter's podcast toolbox additions on to your website designer or developer who will be able to help you.

Sounds complicated: is this worth the effort?

Yes, it is. For many years, Apple mobile devices have led the way in making it easy to consume podcasts. As a result, Apple devices dominate the podcasting space. With Google Podcasts, we think Apple may finally have some meaningful competition in the podcast consumption arena. Google Podcasts looks set to bring podcasting to the masses, using their Android operating system to make podcasts as accessible as they have always been on IOS devices.

SoundCloud

SoundCloud is a great destination on which to host your podcast content. It's popular with a lot of users: many podcasts only publish to SoundCloud as they make consumption of audio as well as hosting your content really easy. We wouldn't recommend being exclusive to SoundCloud, as you miss out on a lot of other great features provided by dedicated podcast hosts but it's a popular audio consumption destination so it's definitely worth the effort to make sure your podcast is available there. We push our content out to SoundCloud via Libsyn, and once set up the publishing is automatic when we publish. Check out the destinations your podcast host will push your content out to and fill out the details for a SoundCloud account so you can hook the two services up.

Additional podcast directories

As well as the larger directories listed above there are a few additional directories which we have found useful in growing our reach. We have listed these in the podcasting toolbox additions at the end of this chapter; be sure to make a note to work through these and check your podcast is listed. Some of them will pull in podcast listing information and RSS feeds from other directories so check you aren't listed already before making a submission.

Social media updates

Posting outposts and updates on social media is a great way to ensure more people hear about your episodes. Very often you will see those interesting topics or fun episodes get picked up by others on social media and shared out to their audiences, which can be a significant source of new listeners for your show. Different social networks will likely have different levels of relevance for your audience. If you are in the business-to-business space, then LinkedIn is a great place to post updates and links to new episodes. Twitter and Facebook have a broad reach for all manner of topics and are worth trying. Don't forget you can further increase your reach by making use of different social platforms' paid boosts and advertising options if you have the budget to support it.

Making use of hashtags

On Twitter, in particular, prudent use of appropriate hashtags can really help your social media updates to travel further afield than your current followers. Not sure which hashtags to use? Take a look at the tool Hashtagify. Just type in the broad topic of your content and Hastagify will suggest potentially related hashtags and give you an idea of which are most commonly used and therefore have the highest potential to help seed your update that little bit further. Just be sure to check how that hashtag is actually being used before you jump in and use it. Hashtags can sometimes have multiple uses for different subjects, and you can end up looking foolish if you crash in on a hashtag inappropriately because you have misunderstood how it's being used. Generally, a search on Twitter for that hashtag should give you the general gist of what it's being used for and its true meaning so you can select appropriately.

Podcast hosting

Dedicated podcast hosting

There are a number of dedicated podcast hosting services and networks you can choose for storing your podcast audio files. If you haven't yet settled on a podcast hosting provider, we have pulled together some of the key players in the podcasting space for you to research and choose. Our own provider of choice is Libsyn, who have always given an amazing service. Having used and benefitted from their services, we can definitely recommend them as a great podcast hosting company.

Why we like Libsyn

One of the best decisions we ever took when starting the *Digital Marketing Podcast* was to choose Libsyn as our podcast hosting provider. Libsyn is currently the largest independent podcast hosting service and has been running since 2004. Their system is easy to use, their technical and customer support are excellent, their servers are reliable, and unlike some other networks and hosting providers, your content always remains your own.

For a modest monthly fee, we are able host and distribute our shows on their servers and get access to great stats on how popular each episode is. They provide a straightforward online interface where we can publish our episodes, and their system takes care of creating the RSS feed that includes all of the standard and proprietary information required by all the major podcast distribution networks. They have built-in integration with a number of key destinations including Spotify, Google Play Music, iHeart Radio, Stitcher and SoundCloud, and continue to add support for additional destinations as they become available.

With Libsyn it's easy to push your content out to multiple sources including Facebook, Twitter, Blogger, WordPress and mobile apps for Apple iOS and Android. They can help you to manage your back catalogue of shows, create a dedicated podcast app for you, and even help you with support for advertising if that's a route you wish to explore.

In common with other good podcast hosting specialists there is no bandwidth limit on your content and there are no fixed contracts that tie you in beyond any individual month. As you grow, if you need more space, you can just choose the next level of hosting. It's really flexible and there really is no limit to how many times your files can be downloaded.

What about other podcast hosting providers?

So clearly we love Libsyn! However, in the interests of remaining objective we have pulled together a few other dedicated podcast hosting providers who also have good reputations for supporting podcasters so you can investigate what they have to offer and explore which might be the best fit for you. Service offerings and prices do change over time, but at the time of writing this book (October 2018), all of these providers had competitively priced services for podcast hosting and fixed monthly flat-rate hosting fee options.

Podcast hosting providers

Blubrry: create.blubrry.com/resources/podcast-media-hosting

Buzzsprout: www.buzzsprout.com

PodBean: www.podbean.com/start-unlimited-podcast

Spreaker: www.spreaker.com

Libsyn: www.libsyn.com

Podcasting toolbox additions

Grammarly: www.grammarly.com

iTunes: www.apple.com/uk/itunes/

Auphonic: auphonic.com

Hashtagify: Hashtagify.com

Submit your podcast for distribution

Podcast Connect: itunesconnect.apple.com/login?module=PodcastsConnect

Spotify for Podcasters: podcasters.spotify.com

Soundcloud: soundcloud.com/for/podcasting

Google Podcasts. For technical guidance on linking your website with Google Podcasts share the following article with your site developer: https://developers.google.com/search/docs/data-types/podcast

Additional podcast directories

Blubrry podcast directory: https://www.blubrry.com/

Stitcher: https://www.stitcher.com/content-providers

Pocket Casts: https://www.pocketcasts.com/submit/

Measuring success

22

Tapping into how and why people listen to your podcast

There are a lot of insights you can draw from your audience. Not all of these will be as robust and complete as many advertisers or marketers would like, but for the podcast producer they can give a fantastic insight into the content you are producing and how audiences consume it. As your audience grows, they will collectively leave behind digital signals that give a sense of what they loved and what they didn't love. Armed with this you can ensure you do more of the stuff they love and less of the things they don't value as highly. The secret is to know where to look and what to look at. So in this chapter that's precisely what we are going to cover.

Podcast host statistics

If you have followed our advice and have set up with a dedicated podcast hosting service, you will likely be given access to some podcast consumption analytics. The examples we are going to give in this section are from our own hosting service Libsyn. Getting a first-hand view of the kind of insights you can get from your show downloads should help you to understand some of what we have been sharing with you on the limitations of podcast measurement. However, by walking you through a combination of different insight sources, we hope to demonstrate how you can take what is available and combine it to create a fuller and more useful picture of how your show is being received and consumed.

What can podcast show statistics tell you?

As all of your show audio files are hosted on your podcast hosting servers, every time an app or service requests a show's MP3 file, specific information is provided back to the podcast hosting service. Hosting companies can tell you how many times each episode file was requested. In most cases, they also record which podcatcher app or podcast directory requested the file to be downloaded. They are even able to pull details of the physical location of the device/user requesting the file. Geographic measurements are limited to countries rather than specific counties or streets, but the information is still useful.

Within our Libsyn dashboard, we have stats organized by each episode (see Figure 22.1). As you can see, the longer each episode has been published, the more downloads that episode will have been able to gather. When trying to determine how large our audience is, we typically look at shows when they have had six to eight weeks to gather downloads. Doing this is slightly arbitrary we know, but we find it is this period that has the majority of show downloads. These statistics were pulled at the start of November 2018, so we can see that our 'Custom Audiences and Retargeting' episode has been a lot more popular in terms of downloads than other episodes published around that time.

We can also get a view of how our overall download numbers are performing by graphing the downloads on a daily basis for a period, as we see in Figure 22.2. Those spikes you see are days when we delivered a new episode. That's the power of having subscribers. Within 48 hours or so of the episode being released, the subscribers' podcatcher software will request and download the file so they can listen to it at a time convenient to them. You have to factor in what time of day you release the episode, otherwise you are not comparing like with like on an episode-by-episode basis. If you want to fine-tune this graph, you are best to schedule your episode releases so they occur at precisely the same time of the day and week each time you publish.

The monthly downloads (see Figure 22.3) will give you a good overview of how your show popularity is growing. Ideally you need to view a broad period of at least 6 to 12 months for it to illustrate long-term trends of growth or decline. Remember these are total downloads you are looking at and will include both the episodes you have released this year and any that have been published in previous years, so this is also showing actions of subscribers digging into your back catalogue of shows. Don't make the mistake of thinking that if you get 40,000

Figure 22.1 Episode download statistics from Libsyn

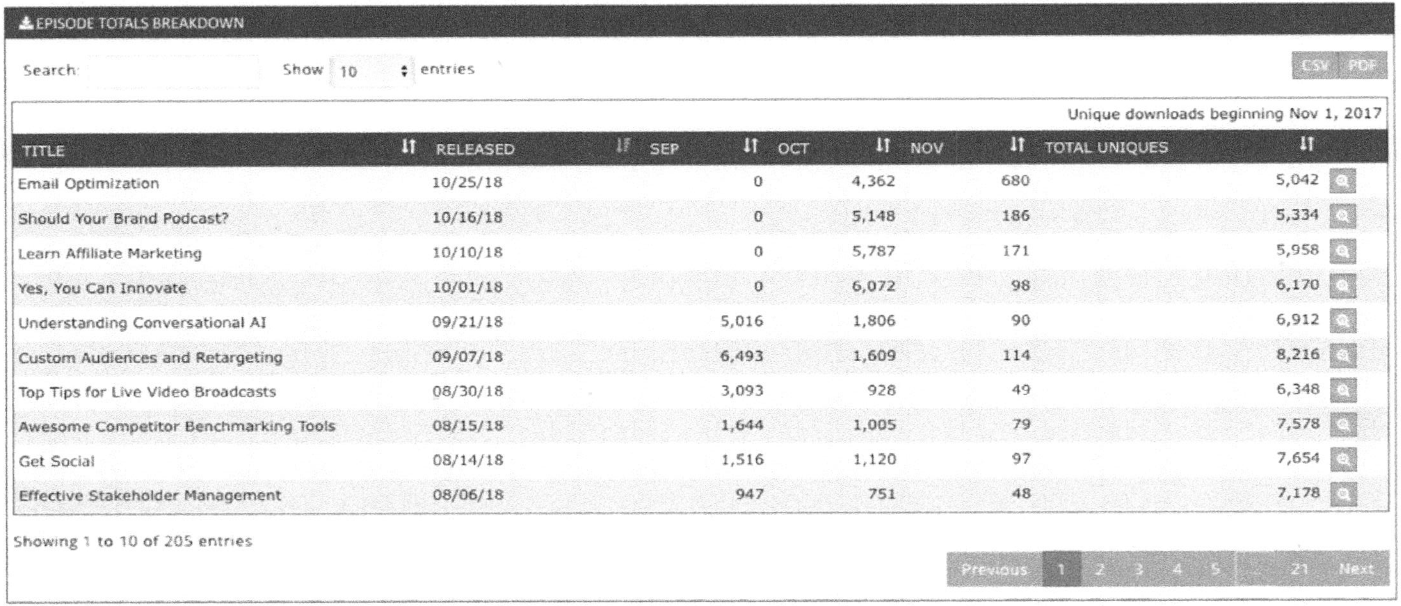

EPISODE TOTALS BREAKDOWN

Search: Show 10 entries

Unique downloads beginning Nov 1, 2017

TITLE	RELEASED	SEP	OCT	NOV	TOTAL UNIQUES	
Email Optimization	10/25/18		0	4,362	680	5,042
Should Your Brand Podcast?	10/16/18		0	5,148	186	5,334
Learn Affiliate Marketing	10/10/18		0	5,787	171	5,958
Yes, You Can Innovate	10/01/18		0	6,072	98	6,170
Understanding Conversational AI	09/21/18		5,016	1,806	90	6,912
Custom Audiences and Retargeting	09/07/18		6,493	1,609	114	8,216
Top Tips for Live Video Broadcasts	08/30/18		3,093	928	49	6,348
Awesome Competitor Benchmarking Tools	08/15/18		1,644	1,005	79	7,578
Get Social	08/14/18		1,516	1,120	97	7,654
Effective Stakeholder Management	08/06/18		947	751	48	7,178

Showing 1 to 10 of 205 entries

Previous 1 2 3 4 5 … 21 Next

Figure 22.2 Daily downloads

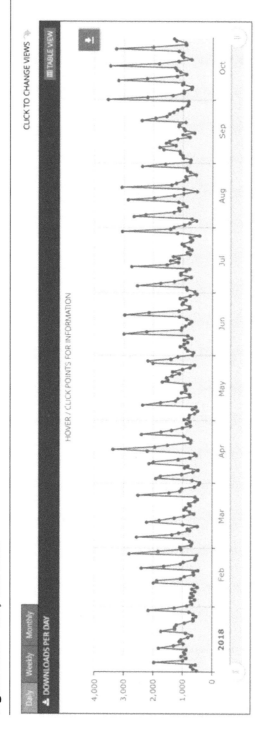

Figure 22.3 Monthly downloads

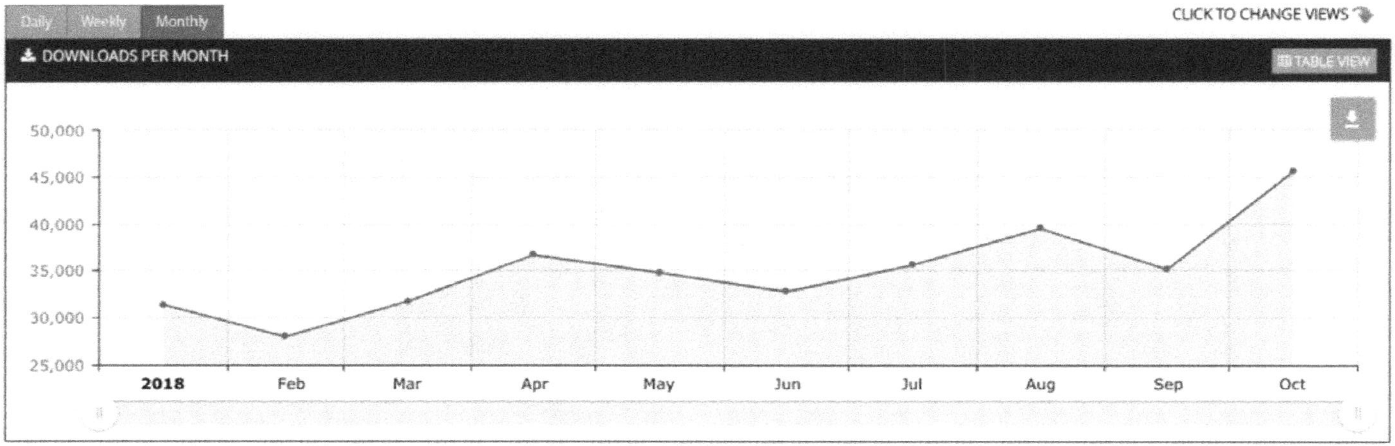

downloads that is how many subscribers you have. Each subscriber can be responsible for many downloads of different episodes in any one month. We have seen a steady increase in 2018 of the number of episodes being downloaded each month. Be aware that if you do increase the frequency at which you release your episodes, it will affect this graph quite dramatically. We haven't increased the frequency of our shows being published, so the month-by-month progression is good to see. When we moved from a fortnightly to a weekly publishing schedule back in 2017, we saw our total download figures double overnight. We still mainly had the same number of subscribers, but we were giving them twice as much content to consume each month.

Figure 22.4 shows the geographic spread of downloads by the location of the listener. You can get a table breakdown of the exact numbers by asking for a table view, but we love the map. It's very slightly interactive. As you roll over each country, it reveals the actual number of downloads for that country for that period. The UK, which we were hovering over when we took this screenshot, has just over half of our total downloads at 105,000 for that period. As an English podcast, our downloads tend to focus on countries where that language is spoken. It's great to monitor how your listeners are growing in different countries. You can even shout out to a particular country and thank the listeners there. We did that once for a handful of our listeners in Burkina Faso in Africa, and they all got back in touch. Never forget these numbers are actual people you have started to build a relationship with. They are all consuming your product, and all of them can spread the word about this free podcast you are giving away if you make it remarkable enough for them.

User agent data (see Figure 22.5) gives you a good idea of why standardization within podcasting is such a challenge. User agent information gives you an indication of what software was used to download the podcast episode. The period we are viewing here had a total of 350,000 downloads, and at least two-thirds of them have come via AppleCoreMedia- or iTunes-related podcatcher apps. The rest are split between over 160 other different user agents. Stitcher and Overcast are essential destinations for us, and a small number of downloads are coming via web browsers such as Chrome, Mozilla and Safari. These views can be influenced by sharing of your content in social media as often those links will point to the embeddable show player on your website. It's worth keeping an eye on any growth in these browser user agents for episodes because it can help to indicate how your social outreach is working. That said, you can get a much fuller picture of what your website activity is generating by looking at Google Analytics if you have that set up; we will explore this in a lot more detail in Chapter 24.

Figure 22.4 Geographic spread

Figure 22.5   User agents

🔽 DOWNLOADS PER USER AGENT	
TITLE ⇅	DOWNLOADS ⬇
AppleCoreMedia	206,789
Stitcher	25,122
iTunes	24,154
itunesstored	16,902
Overcast	11,934
CastBox	8,556
Chrome	8,283
okhttp	8,135
Mozilla	5,368
Pocket Casts	3,611

Search: _____   Show 10 ⇕ entries   CSV PDF

Showing 1 to 10 of 166 entries

Previous 1 2 3 4 5 … 17 Next

Spotify stats

The one destination you won't see any download stats for in your main Libsyn stats is Spotify. Spotify works slightly differently to other podcatcher software. They store the files for your show separately on Spotify servers, so the stats are split out. Spotify is a relatively new destination for us. We launched there back in November 2017 and have seen a steady growth of listeners but it's relatively small for our show at around 300–400 downloads a month. We saw a drop-off in July to September, which could mean we pushed out content the Spotify audience didn't like so much, or it could be a reflection of the younger audience we know we have there. We teach digital marketing at a number of UK universities and know a lot of our students listen via Spotify because they tell us. It does highlight the fact that there isn't much detail to go on when you notice dips or growth in your show figures. You have to do quite a bit of guessing and hypothesizing to paint a picture.

So that's about it regarding what show download stats can indicate. But our storytelling journey doesn't end there. There are other sources of data about your audience you can pull on. None of them are as complete as your show download stats, but they can shed more light on what users are engaging with.

Apple's Podcast Connect

If you want more detail on how your audience responds to an individual episode, it can be handy to check out the data for that month in Apple's Podcast Connect. Podcast Connect is where you can let Apple know you have a podcast you'd like shared. You sign into the service using an Apple ID. If you already have one you can use this, but do bear in mind that once you submit your podcast, that podcast will be tied into your Apple ID. If you are setting up a podcast for another brand or company, you may do well to create a new Apple ID to manage your podcast publishing. You can submit multiple podcasts to Apple if you have more than one show. Any shows submitted will be visible in your 'my podcasts' tab.

Submitting a podcast is relatively simple. You need to provide Apple with the URL of your RSS feed. Feeds submitted have to conform to the RSS 2.0 spec and contain podcast artwork at least 1400 x 1400 pixels formatted as JPG or PNG in the RGB colour space.

Once you have submitted, you then have to wait and keep a close eye on the status of the feed, which will show as either Prepared for Submission, Submitted for Review, Active, Rejected, Hidden or Failed Validation. Once your status shows as active, your podcast is available via Apple Podcasts and iTunes. This can take a while to happen, particularly in the lead-up to Christmas and the new year. That's why having an episode zero is such a great idea. It enables you to get listed in advance of releasing your first show so that when you do launch, you are available to listeners where it matters.

Podcast Connect analytics

As well as being the location where you launch your show for Apple device audiences, Podcast Connect includes a handy analytics service. It launched back in the autumn of 2017 and it's really useful. You can view data on show downloads over the last 60 days. It's not a complete view of your show's consumption; the data only reports on devices with iOS 11 or iTunes

12.7 or later, and Apple HomePod devices. Apple also provides a handy note to say that the data can be delayed for up to 72 hours. So anyone on an IOS device running an OS version before IOS 11 or iTunes 12.7 isn't going to show up here. This is slightly frustrating, we know, but hats off to Apple for including the functionality in their software to give this kind of feedback. In podcatching software terms it was a bit of a first as far as we are aware and it's very insightful. Being a sample audience, the figures here are not going to correlate with your overall download stats so it's best to think of this as a bit of a focus group that can give you a sample insight on what your audience wants to consume.

What does this focus group share with you?

For each episode you get an overview of the duration of each show, the number of devices that downloaded it, the total time listened to, time per device and average percentage of that show's consumption. You also get a convenient breakdown of how many people in this sample audience are subscribed, and how many aren't subscribed but have dipped into an episode. For our show, this is currently at 77 per cent subscribed/23 per cent not subscribed. Just keeping an eye on these metrics can be revealing.

Until Apple launched this service, we had no idea how much of each show our audience listened to. What podcast connect analytics has taught us is that the length of the show does matter to a significant portion of our audience. The sweet spot according to our Podcast Connect listeners' behaviour is around 25 minutes or under, and we achieve a healthy 70–85 per cent of the episode being listened to. When we go beyond that to, say, 30 minutes plus, the number consistently drops to an average of around 50 per cent of the show content being consumed. Initially we wondered if length was the key factor here, but another pattern came to light. Our longer episodes are always interviews with different experts and our shorter episodes are all shows with just the two of us hosting. Length could be a problem, but more likely there is something about our Daniel and Ciaran shows they enjoy. Shorter interview shows definitely perform better so we may need to adjust the format on future interviews to keep them more concise. To really test this out we should probably run some joint chat shows of over 30 minutes to see how our audience reacts. The lesson here is to look harder at the data before you jump to conclusions about the patterns you are seeing. Experiment and learn.

Individual episode details

The insights don't stop there. If you want to get a view of how long your listeners kept with an individual episode you can drill down into the analytics at a show level. Show level analytics gives you a timeline of the show with the corresponding percentage of listeners who made it through the show at any point. You can play the audio of the show in this report and see how the audience kept with it. Any sharp drop-offs in your listener graph should be listened to so you can learn what it was that occurred at the point you lost some of their attention. Ideally, you will need a large enough sample audience to get an insight into the wisdom of your crowd. Percentages based on small numbers can, as we all know, be misleading, but once you can regularly get around 100 devices per episode into Podcast Connect analytics you gain a precious tool for audience feedback.

Podcast reviews

One of the best sources of listener feedback you can get is podcast reviews. Apple's listing for your podcast in iTunes will more than likely be the primary source of these, but other services that list your podcast can include listener reviews as well. We have always encouraged listeners to leave us reviews in iTunes. It's so helpful to get both good and bad feedback; without it, you do often find yourself wondering why you slave away on your show month after month. We suspect that new reviews may well help shows to be ranked and listed in iTunes' 'What's hot' listings. Actual downloads over a 60-day period matter a lot as well for these listings but as far as we can tell reviews also give you a boost.

Finding your reviews

iTunes doesn't flag up for you when you have a new review so you will want to make sure you have a copy of iTunes and regularly check your show for new reviews and ratings. In iTunes, go to the store and search for your podcast name. You should get to a page listing your show artwork graphic and all of your episodes. Next to each episode you will see the time duration, date of release and the short description you submitted to your RSS feed. The popularity bar next to each episode indicates how popular that show is based on the previous 60 days of downloads. If you want to see your ratings and reviews, click on the tab labelled 'Ratings and Reviews' between the 'Details' and 'Related' links to the right of your show artwork. Organize the reviews by most recent, and you get to see the most recent reviews for your show. Great, right? Everything all in one place. Well, actually, that's not the case! When you use the iTunes store, you are logged into a particular country's version of the store. If you scroll right to the bottom of your reviews page, you will find on the right-hand side a country flag icon. That will tell you which country's store you are viewing. If you want to see reviews left by listeners in other countries, you will have to click on specific flag icons and navigate to different national iTunes stores. We only recently discovered this. Suddenly we found an additional 60 or so reviews we never knew we had. Some were good, some were pointing out ways to improve, but all of them fabulously useful.

Monitoring reviews

Monitoring multiple iTunes reviews from multiple countries isn't the most efficient way of getting your review data. Fortunately, there is an excellent tool that can pull them all into one place for you and it's called My Podcast Reviews. My Podcast Reviews will pull in all the reviews from both iTunes and Stitcher that they find online. They offer a free account for those just wanting to try the tool out, which gives you the most recent 30 reviews, but their premium paid-for accounts give you access to a full archive of reviews for your show. Depending on the level of subscription you choose you can get monthly, weekly or daily updated reports on reviews. It's a huge time-saver and we love the weekly updates it gives us with only new reviews we haven't seen before.

Learning from your reviews

The number of reviews you receive will always be tiny in relation to your total download numbers, but that doesn't in any way undermine how useful they are. Listeners who do speak up are well worth listening to. If one listener is thinking about an aspect of your show that they feel the need to share, whether it's positive or negative, you can be sure lots of other listeners feel the same way. You can't see the name of the reviewer, just their chosen iTunes review username. Giving those usernames a shout out on your show for their feedback is an excellent way of not only rewarding those listeners but of also creating a sense of a community and belonging. We don't know precisely who 'Angry pig-killing chick' is, but can deduce she was a fan at some stage of the game Angry Birds. However, we loved the review she sent us, and when we give her a shout out she will definitely know who we are thanking. With each shout out, you will see additional listeners thinking, 'Hey... that's cool. I wonder if I leave a review they will shout out to me?' It's a technique we have been experimenting with recently, and it definitely works.

If anyone is overly harsh in their review, don't take it to heart. Try to take a step back and ponder what you can proactively do about it. We had one quite recently that said, 'How many "actuallys" can you get into a podcast... my ears are bleeding! Aaaahhhh!!!' It made us laugh, but behind the ribbing was a cautious nudge that we perhaps had overused that word in previous episodes. Aware that it grates on at least one listener's earbuds, we will be more aware of that verbal tick moving forward. Mmnw1985 if you are reading this... thanks for letting us know and for the three stars you gave us along with it. It was much appreciated.

Many of our reviews focus on the short, concise format we follow, which helps to reinforce what we have seen in our Podcast Connect analytics. We have also had really useful feedback on sound quality, which has caused us to review how we are recording and editing. We also get great insight into where a lot of our listeners consume the podcast. Walking the dog, working out at the gym, listening on the daily commute are all quite common references in our reviews, which again helps to explain why overall our audience engages well with content under half an hour long. Read your reviews as they are written and over time you will be able to gain some very useful insights into common traits shared by your audience. Somehow it really helps to be able to picture them as we create further content. It certainly helps to almost put a face to the download numbers and stats.

Google Analytics

If you have a website for your podcast, it is well worth setting up Google Analytics so you can get some insight into the show's website traffic. Google Analytics is a free-to-use system that can measure and monitor visitor traffic on your website. It can give you an insight into which of your show pages are getting traffic and how long visitors are staying there. It isn't a great way to analyse the popularity of your episodes on its own, as most listeners won't be using the website to listen to your show. However, it can monitor your website and see how the site's audience reacts to the content you place there. When you post out updates on social media, having a web page where your episodes live can be a great way to direct new listeners to your show. If Google Analytics looks too overwhelming, then make sure your first stop is Google's Analytics Academy. There you will find some great step-by-step video tutorials on how to get set up and started. We have included a link for you in this chapter's podcast toolkit additions section. For those of you into Google Analytics and all the great stuff you can learn from it, take a dive into Chapter 24, where we explore how it can be used in more detail.

Drawing conclusions

Using a mixture of reviews, show download stats and Podcast Connect analytics you really can start to draw some conclusions about your audience and how they are consuming and reacting to the content you publish. The key to getting the most from this is to keep an open mind and continually ask both 'Why?' and 'So what are we going to do with this/or as a result of this information?' to each pattern or trend you spot. Ask both of these questions regularly enough and over time you will improve and refine what you have to offer your audience. It's a cliché we know, but celebrate your successes and take any knocks you receive along the way on the chin, safe in the knowledge that each one will make you stronger.

Podcasting toolbox additions

Google Analytics: https://analytics.google.com
Google Analytics Academy: https://analytics.google.com/analytics/academy/
Podcast Connect: https://itunesconnect.apple.com/login?module=Podcasts vConnect
My Podcast Reviews: https://mypodcastreviews.com

The podcast marketing toolkit

23

In this chapter, we'll explore a range of techniques including social media channels, influencer and advocate outreach, display advertising, email marketing and paid search. The main missing digital channel is Search Engine Optimization, which we've already covered when we talked about landing pages.

1 Social media

Social media has had the greatest impact on branding of any of the digital 'channels' we discuss in this section. Actually, calling social media a channel doesn't put it in perspective properly. Social media has fundamentally changed how we engage and interact with brands and has led to the shift in marketing that podcasting is very much part of.

The fundamental shift has been towards two-way communications and empowerment of the consumer (in both B2C and B2B contexts). Through social media, rather than just broadcasting *at* you, I can engage *with* you. If you take any of the traditional branding metrics such as awareness and recall, brand awareness is the extent to which a brand is recognized by potential customers; brand recall is when a brand is correctly associated with a particular product, branding or characteristic. Customers are far more likely to be impacted by 'engaging with' than they are by just 'listening to' something, so by using social media hand in hand with my podcast content, I have a winning combination. However, engagement takes effort, so you first need to provide value in order to get them to engage. That value may take many forms, but podcast content is ideal, so your already engaged audience now has not only valuable content, but also somewhere they can interact with its creators and the rest of the audience.

Social is personal

What we need to consider is how to best utilize this social behaviour for our organizations to help achieve our podcasting objectives while providing value and without interrupting an individual's private and personal space. Social users are increasingly cautious about how they use social media. With a 66 per cent drop in trust in Facebook (Weisbaum, 2018) happening after a single data breach (albeit a very large one), we can see how acutely users are concerned about how their data is being used. That means as podcasters, we need to adopt a considered approach to how we use social media to build and engage with our audiences.

User journey and value proposition

Two of the main themes that we discussed in previous chapters were understanding the user journey and considering our value proposition. These considerations are key to using social media effectively. We need to make sure that we understand which social platforms our target audience is using and that when they use these platforms the user experience provides value. Too much social media activity is carried out just for the sake of activity.

Content and engagement

Our ability to utilize social media effectively will come down to having interesting and useful content to share, and being willing and able to engage in an open and authentic way. Because of the personal nature of social media, a standard 'corporate communications' tone doesn't work. Even in a B2B environment, we are still dealing with individuals and need to apply core social media principles to our communications.

Bear in mind that anyone can blog or post to social media sites, but it doesn't mean anyone is listening. However, with podcast audiences being highly engaged, they offer an ideal opportunity to use social media to build engagement. Our podcasts are fantastic content in their own right, and are ideal for sharing via social media.

Podcast as content and engagement driver

So how can podcasts sit at the heart of our social strategy? Essentially podcasts are great content, and sharing entire podcasts, podcast clips and excerpts from interviews are all great ways of providing value via our social channels.

Social also then allows us to engage with our audience via these channels, and our podcasts can be used to signpost people back to the social channels we use. So, for example, we could set up private social groups on LinkedIn or Facebook, for example, to give our audience an exclusive destination just for them. This can help build a real sense of community and peer-to-peer engagement, as well as being a great place to get feedback.

Outreach, engagement and ego

To really get the most from our podcasts, we should always consider how we can maximize our reach into our target audience. Social outreach and engagement is a highly effective way of doing this, and as well as increasing the size of our audience it can help us to create positive engagement.

If I keep on publishing useful and engaging podcast content, regularly update my social channels and positively engage with anyone who leaves comments or feedback, I will gradually grow my social media audience. If, however, I want to speed up this process and create the maximum amplification for my efforts then I am going to need to focus on social media outreach.

Social media outreach is all about identifying the key influencers and advocates within a particular group. If I can get these key people to share my updates and podcast episodes, then I can amplify my visibility and potentially grow my audience.

So let's define what we mean by an influencer or an advocate.

Advocates are the easiest group to identify as they are those people who leave positive comments, share podcast episodes and generally engage in a positive way. They are willing to spread what you say and add to your social voice. They are our greatest asset and we need to engage, encourage and reward this group in order to build loyalty.

Influencers are those people with access to the audience that we want to influence. We can use social media tools to identify them and we then need a strategy to get engagement and encourage them to become advocates.

Judging influence

You can use a number of measures to judge influence online. You could look at the number of social connections that someone has, or at the quality of their audience. You could consider how likely it is that what they say will be read and repeated. This process can be quite time-consuming and therefore it is worth considering some of the key tools that can help us understand influence.

Klear aims to take the pain away from trying to work out levels of influence online. It works by looking at a range of social platforms, assessing a range of different factors, such as your likelihood of being re-tweeted, and then gives you a score out of 100. It will also assign topics that it believes you are influential about and show if you are in the top percentage of influencers.

The key point of Klear is that it provides a nice, easy metric to initially assess influence – you can then dig a little deeper and plan your outreach campaigns by seeing what kinds of content people are sharing. For example, I have a plug-in for Google Chrome that shows me the Klear scores of all the influential people whose tweets I am reading on Twitter, and I can use Twitter as an interface to search for influencers on any topic. That way I can see who is most influential and can prioritize my engagement activities accordingly.

Another approach to judging social influence is to use a social monitoring tool that helps you to identify the most influential users on a particular platform.

Brand, social media, online PR and search optimization

It is important to understand that there is a very close connection between your social media activity, Public Relations (PR) activity and search optimization. It is also essential to realize that all of these things make up a significant part of your digital branding. We will look at search in more detail in the next chapter, but the effectiveness of your social media activity will create 'social signals' that influence your search rankings (essential to the quantity and quality of conversation that is happening in social media around your topics of interest).

Social engagement and outreach are essentially online PR, but your offline PR activities can also impact what you talk about in social media and how many people are linking to your sites and social media platforms. For this reason, we need everyone involved in these three disciplines to be working collaboratively and to be aware of what the others are doing.

Social measurement

The greatest mistake made in a huge number of organizations (in my experience the majority) is to focus on volume-based metrics when looking at social media campaigns. More often than not, a campaign is started and the initial target is to reach a certain number of likes or followers. But, in reality, what does having a million followers actually mean? The answer is very little. We need to understand who that audience is, look at how engaged they are, their sentiment and, most importantly, understand if social media is actually having an impact on your business objectives.

We can use analytics in a number of ways to look at the success of our social media effects. We can start with the basics and look at how much traffic we get from social media sites to our websites. We could then take it a stage further and look at how many of these visits are on mobile devices. If you are using analytics effectively, you will also have set up goals, and you can see what part social media is having on driving your website visitors to complete your goals. All of this will be covered in more detail in the next chapter, but the key point to remember here is that it's not just about the social media data, such as number of followers or amount of engagement, it is actually about understanding how this drives your end objectives.

Sentiment analysis

Many social media tools will carry out some form of sentiment analysis. The idea is that the context of the social media mentions that you receive is analysed, and the sentiment or intention of the social media user is understood. This most usually takes the form of grouping these mentions into positive, negative and neutral.

There is a problem, however. The majority of social media tools get this completely wrong. These tools work by looking at the text and using fairly rudimentary methods of analysing the language. For example, if I tweet 'Top 10 digital marketing disasters of 2018' and then link to my website, many tools will see this as a negative tweet and associate negativity with the link to my website. It will be seen as negative due to the use of the word 'disasters', even though from experience I know that this will actually be a very popular tweet. Some tools, however, are a lot more effective at analysing language and take a far more sophisticated approach. These tools certainly aren't 100 per cent accurate, but they are far less likely to make rudimentary mistakes like this.

The solution is to understand how effective your particular tool is at analysing the social platforms you are looking at, and then manually check the results you get. This doesn't mean reading every single tweet or comment (although in an ideal world you will), but it certainly means scanning through and understanding the assumption that the tool is making.

This is particularly important when you look at 'share of voice'. During a really bad social media crisis, when everyone is talking about you and saying negative things, your share of voice will be high. You therefore need to understand sentiment when you look at share of voice.

Social media advertising

Many social media platforms give you a number of paid advertising options. We need to discuss the implications of paid social campaigns here, however, as they can heavily impact the effectiveness and measurement of your social campaigns.

Value proposition, privacy and trust

Since social media is very much part of our personal lives in many cases, we need to be very cautious about how we use it in a commercial way. Almost everything we have spoken about so far involves providing value via engagement and understanding the user's needs. Exactly the same principle should be applied to social media advertising.

We need to consider how much of an interruption social advertising can actually be seen as, how it can actually damage our brands if used badly and what image of our organization we are projecting.

The key point is to understand the social platforms you are using, why a user is there and to make sure that the value proposition is clear. If you are on Facebook and you are interested in health and fitness, and a brand such as Nike offers you a podcast to help you achieve your fitness goals, then that's great. If, however, you are on Facebook and you have liked a digital marketing podcast, it doesn't mean that any of your friends necessarily have an interest in it.

Trusting algorithms

It is actually in Facebook's interest not to annoy people with irrelevant ads, just as it is not good for Google to give you irrelevant search results. Both scenarios lead to dissatisfied users, which in turn leads to those users moving to other social networks and search engines.

The algorithms – which are just sets of rules and logic – behind these sites are what decide on what ads you are shown or what search results you are given. Google has spent many years and much investment developing its algorithms and focusing on relevancy. The Facebook algorithm filters out content that it thinks isn't relevant to the user and re-orders other content based on how relevant it appears to be. However, it also means that Facebook is able to sell advertising due to organizations not necessarily being able to get their content in front of their audience for free. 'Organic reach' is the consequence of this algorithm, and your organic reach is the percentage of people that have liked your page on Facebook, who actually see your content. The average organic reach for a wide range of the organizations I work with is currently 1 per cent. This basically means that so few people actually see your content, even though they have liked your page, you need to pay for additional visibility.

Social media conclusions

As well as needing to consider all of the usual complexities of social media when planning our podcast content, we have some additional things to take into account. We still need to consider appropriate use of channels, focus on content and engagement, and find effective measurement strategies. Most importantly with podcasts, we need to consider how they fit in with overall user experience and be very clearly focused on transparency and trust.

The overall user experience is all down to making sure we have thought through and tested how the user will actually experience our podcast content and how they can engage with us. Although time-consuming and fragmented, due to the number of social platforms and scenarios involved, it is a very practical and reasonably straightforward issue.

Trust, on the other hand, is far more subjective but is of huge importance. Social media can act as a magnifier for missteps we make as marketers. By interrupting, being irrelevant or making incorrect assumptions we will actually inconvenience our target audience. This may be by giving them irrelevant content to fast-forward past, or bombarding them with the same episode again and again.

A well-planned and strategic approach to social media will not only make best use of the tools and channels available, but will do so with a view on how this makes up part of the broader user journey. If we want to grow and build advocacy with our podcast audiences, social media gives us huge opportunities, and the risks can be mitigated if we follow a well-thought-out social process.

2 Online advertising

If we want to build an audience for a podcast, online advertising offers us a fantastic opportunity to reach a targeted audience quickly and easily. Also, thanks to podcasts offering value for free, and generally being part of the early stages of the user journey, they lend themselves incredibly well to being promoted in display ads across the web.

However, online advertising is also probably the easiest aspect of digital marketing to waste your budget on by carrying out ineffective campaigns. Banner ads are the easiest part of our digital marketing to understand from a traditional advertising perspective, which means that many traditional marketers' approach to digital has been to create print/TV ads and then create digital equivalents of these in a banner format. This approach is generally poorly targeted and not adjusted accordingly for the digital channel it is delivered through. Much of the blame for this lies with agencies that don't really understand digital, but also because it is a channel that lends itself to a 'broadcast' approach. I have said that justifying marketing activity for which we can calculate the return is often put down to 'brand building' and this has been particularly true of banner ads. As click-through rates go down, we persuade ourselves that it is not about the click, but we do little to measure its effectiveness.

The positive side of online advertising is that we now have a wide range of creative and targeting options that can improve the effectiveness of our ads, along with the analytics and metrics to judge their success.

Advertising objectives

Just like any other aspect of our podcast marketing we should start by clearly defining what our actual end objectives are and how online advertising is going to contribute to these goals. This is even more important to define when considering online ads because of the way they are often priced and measured.

Much online advertising is sold on a cost per mille (CPM) basis. This basically means that you pay a certain fee every time your ad is shown 1,000 times, so you are paying for display, not even clicks, and certainly not for results. This isn't the only option, but it is common. The result is that it is very easy to waste budget on views of your ad that are seen by the completely wrong audience.

Your ad being shown once is called an 'impression'. If I hit refresh 10 times on a page with an ad on it, that will be 10 ad impressions. Also, if a page loads that my ad is on, but the ad is below the fold (below the part of the page that I can see without scrolling down), and the user doesn't scroll down the page, the ad will still have had an impression even though no one saw it. The impression also doesn't tell you how long the user was actually on the page that the ad was shown on. This page view duration is referred to as 'dwell time', and even if my dwell time was half a second, if the ad loaded, an impression gets counted. We clearly need to look carefully at what we are paying for.

Another challenge with online advertising is that results are often measured on a click-through rate (CTR) basis. The reality, though, is that even if we get clicks it doesn't mean that the visitor who drives to your site will necessarily listen to or subscribe to your podcast. They may leave your site as soon as they arrive on the landing page. Equally, someone who doesn't click on your ads may become aware of your podcast and go on to search for it in Google. This means that we need to find better ways than CTR to measure the success of an ad.

App advertising

As well as the options for advertising on mobile sites, we also need to consider ads within apps. This may be from the perspective of running ad campaigns in appropriate apps that are used by your target audience, but it may be from the perspective of making money by placing ads within your apps.

On both iOS and Android you can integrate ads from a wide variety of different ad networks (more on this later). All of these solutions generally work by automatically placing ads within your apps (in the locations you have developed into the app) and then giving you a share of the revenue made from the ads.

If you want to advertise within apps, then there are a number of different ad networks you could go to (again, more on this later) or you could approach an app owner directly to negotiate a deal.

Ad networks versus media owners

An ad network manages the advertising space on a number of different locations that may include both websites and apps. They offer a range of targeting options and then place your ads within the sites/apps they manage according to your targeting criteria. Different ad networks have different targeting criteria, which can vary from fairly basic options such as category matching (automotive, finance, etc) all the way through to things such as behavioural targeting.

Generally, ad networks charge a fee and then share some of this with the owner of the location where the ads are shown. They provide the technology for placing the ads, the account management to the advertisers, and provide some form of reporting for all parties involved.

Ad networks are why there are standard sizes and types of ads. This means you can create an ad once and it can be run across multiple properties (mobile sites and apps) without the need to redesign every time.

Rather than going to an ad network, you could go directly to a media owner. A media owner is someone who owns a site or app (or even email list) that you may wish to advertise on. Going directly to a media owner has the advantage of knowing exactly where and how your ads will be shown (this often isn't true when using ad networks, because some ad placement is 'blind', meaning you set the targeting criteria but don't get to choose the exact sites that your ads show on). The disadvantage of going direct is that very often you are targeting one site or app at a time and they don't have the targeting technologies available via the ad networks. They may also be limited in the types of creative options they offer and the reporting facilities they provide.

Targeting options

Different ad networks offer different types of ad targeting, and I've summarized the most common of these below. One network normally doesn't offer all of the options, and different networks will have access to place advertising on different websites. Thus you may need to work with multiple ad networks to achieve your campaign objectives. The most common types of targeting are:

Location: place your ads using location-based criteria such as country, city and distance from a physical location. This option can often also be used to exclude as well as include an area.

Demographic: target by criteria such as age and gender. This may be based on users who have registered their details or it may be based on some sort of modelling basis, in which case it is worth understanding how this data is modelled and how likely the data is to be accurate.

Category: one of the simplest forms of targeting, this is based on the category of the content within the site or app, for example, automotive, finance, etc.

Content matched: the content of the page the ad is being placed on is read and ads are matched based on content. This is how ads are placed within Google's display network. This can be effective, but just because I am reading a news story about pirates doesn't mean I want to buy a boat!

Behavioural: there are lots of different approaches to behavioural targeting, but generally these rely on being able to see a user's behaviour across a website (or number of websites) and then targeting ads accordingly. I may be looking at an automotive website, but if I have just been on three websites looking at credit card deals, then it is perfectly valid to show me an ad for a credit card on the automotive website.

Re-targeting: this allows you to show ads to users who have visited your site before. So, for example, if I visit your site but don't buy anything, I could then be shown ads for your site on other websites.

Creative options

This is where things start to get very interesting. The amount of different creative options for display ads is exploding. A few of the more common options are listed below, along with a pointer to where to find some great resources for getting creative inspiration (a black-and-white book doesn't really do interactive online advertising full justice!):

Banners: images can be displayed with or without animation, and users can tap the banner to be taken to a variety of destinations.

Expandable: expands an ad to cover the full screen upon a tap, without removing the user from the app or mobile browser experience.

Interstitial: displays full-screen rich media ads either at app or mobile browser launch or in between content pages.

Video: various options to place video before/after/during other video content or within other rich media formats.

Mobile: a wide range of ad creatives are fully optimized for mobile and the small amount of display space that is available.

https://www.richmediagallery.com/

Ad reporting and analytics

Most ad networks will provide reporting tools, but ideally we should integrate our advertising data with our mobile and app analytics so that we can get an integrated view of our mobile marketing efforts.

An initial step is to make sure that all of our mobile ads are tagged with analytics tracking code. This allows us to identify any traffic coming from our mobile ads to our sites and apps and then track this through to conversion.

Taking things a stage further, Google now allows you to import data from other ad networks and platforms into Google Analytics so that you can compare and contrast data in one place.

Online advertising conclusions

The display advertising market is currently highly fragmented, with a huge range of ad targeting, features and creative options that can help build our podcast audiences. Just like any form of advertising, the results of campaigns are highly variable based on the options used and the overall effectiveness of approach. For this reason, any online advertising efforts should be carefully considered and tied back to business objectives, with a clear methodology put in place from the outset for tracking and measuring results.

The varied, and often highly interactive, creative options available are very impressive. However, if we go back to our initial concerns about user objectives, we need to ask some very searching questions before making assumptions about the effectiveness of any online advertising campaigns.

It is very easy to be sold online advertising on the basis of its 'brand impact'. Don't forget it is one of many touchpoints and, as the easiest to understand from a traditional advertising and branding point of view, it is often over-relied on. Map out the user journey, work out where it fits in and then measure for success.

3 Email marketing

One of the greatest challenges of podcasting is that we know how many listeners we have by using podcast statistics publishing tools like Libsyn, but we don't know who these people are. Email sign-ups are an ideal way in which to collect data and build a bit more understanding about our audience.

Focusing on the user

In this section we'll look at each element of email marketing in turn, but we need to keep our target podcast audience at the heart of this journey. Bear in mind your ability to target, personalize and maximize the impact of your emails will be greatly affected by your email service provider (ESP). Some of the most popular and low-cost ESPs, such as Mailchimp, are increasingly offering a wide range of services useful to podcasters well beyond just basic email campaigns.

It's also worth stating at this point that email marketing is getting harder. We are all increasingly likely to not open newsletters, and we are all getting more and more email (MacDonald, 2019). Email marketing is the easiest digital channel to do badly; even the industry language of 'emails blasts' sums this up. So, if we are to do email marketing we need to do it well and provide value with the content we send.

Ease of iteration

The single greatest thing about email, in my opinion, is the ability to test, learn and change quickly and easily. Trying different versions of pages on your website or creating different apps can be expensive, time-consuming and often fraught with technical problems. Trying different email subject lines, calls to action or length of copy are all extremely easy things to test, assuming you are using the right ESP.

An ESP will allow you to store email lists, create and send email campaigns and track results for you, and how well suited your ESP is to your needs will have a direct impact on how effective your email campaigns can be. There are dozens of different ESPs out there, ranging from the basic through to highly sophisticated systems that could be used as CRM systems in their own right. We'll explore what we need from an ESP in more detail in a moment, but first we need to look at the state of the email market and dispel some myths.

The decline of spam and rise of Bacn

You are probably very aware of the concept of spam, defined as unsolicited email communications. As we have said, spam is actually on the decrease and a range of security and technology solutions are helping to progress this fight. What is generally on the rise, though, is Bacn (pronounced bacon)! Bacn is defined as the range of emails that we have signed up for but don't see as relevant and never read. Over time we subscribe to more and more newsletters, we get service and social media updates we never read and are generally getting more email which, although not truly spam, isn't relevant or useful to us.

Increasingly, webmail clients like Gmail are trying to separate this kind of email from those that are relevant by placing them under separate tabs. Different systems have different ways of judging the relevance of an email, but very often it is based on user behaviour. If you regularly open and click on email from a particular address, these systems will learn your behaviour, identify that an email is relevant and place it in your main inbox. Therefore, getting engagement and clicks on every one of your emails becomes even more important as it will impact whether your future emails are seen.

There also services like Sanebox.com that can help filter our email, unsubscribe from unwanted newsletters and summarize lower-priority content. All of this means that if our emails aren't seen to provide value, our target audiences just won't see them in the first place.

Focusing on relevance

This movement toward separating essential emails from promotional ones means that if we use email as a broadcast channel, focusing sales messages, we are likely to get lower and lower response rates. The nature of mobile users trying to 'triage' their email means we have precious few seconds to demonstrate the value of our content. We need to focus on using a range of techniques and technologies available to us to make our email as tailored, relevant and useful as possible to our audience, and that's what we'll explore in this chapter.

This doesn't mean that you can't send promotional emails with products and special offers. If I ask you to send me special offers that's what you should do, but they need to be the right offers for me sent at the right time at the right level of frequency. And if I've signed up for a newsletter, don't just send me sales messages. The general approach I apply to email marketing when not working on an e-commerce basis, and an immediate online sale is not the proposed outcome, is to consider the principles of content marketing. There should be a ratio of commercial and non-commercial content in your emails, and by that I mean really providing value through your email content. Many of my clients work on an 80/20 rule, that is 80 per cent non-commercial useful content, and 20 per cent about stuff they want to sell you. I'd suggest you go even further and aim for a 90/10 or 100 per cent non-commercial content. Providing useful content is the single best way to get your email known and remembered, increase the likelihood of future email opens and drive traffic to your site. Once you have the site visitor, you have the opportunity to build trust, awareness and potentially drive them along your sales funnel.

Email and the user journey

Once we understand the impact email marketing has on our potential user journey and how effectively it can work as one of our digital touchpoints we can start to really look at the great return on investment email marketing can offer. Essentially we need to add an email sign-up to a point in the user journey and incentivize sign-up with exclusive content or early access to podcasts not available elsewhere.

The importance of tracking code

When we look at our web analytics to try to understand where our web traffic is coming from and how it is impacting our bottom line, our traffic sources are an essential report. In Google Analytics these are found under the Acquisition reports and are broken down into some key areas. Organic search is traffic from sites like Google (but not paid advertising from these sites), Referrals are visits from other websites, Social is visits from social websites, and then we come to Direct visits. Supposedly, direct traffic is traffic that comes to your site when somebody types your web address directly into their browser or has bookmarked your site and visits by selecting that bookmark. What direct traffic actual represents is visits that your analytics package has no idea where they have come from.

This is a really important thing to understand in regard to email, because unless we add tracking code (which we'll explain in a moment and cover in more detail in the next chapter) to the links in our emails, then people clicking on these links will show up as direct traffic and we won't be able to differentiate where they came from. So when we send out our email campaigns, we'll see an increase in direct traffic, but we couldn't 100 per cent identify that as being from our email.

Tracking code basically involves adding some information to each of our links, so when a visitor arrives on our site we can use our analytics to identify exactly where they have come from. You can see the Google URL builder that allows us to generate this code in Figure 23.1 and see Chapter 24 on measurement to learn more about it. It is also possible that your ESP gives the option to automatically add tracking code, which can be a great time saver.

Figure 23.1   Google URL builder

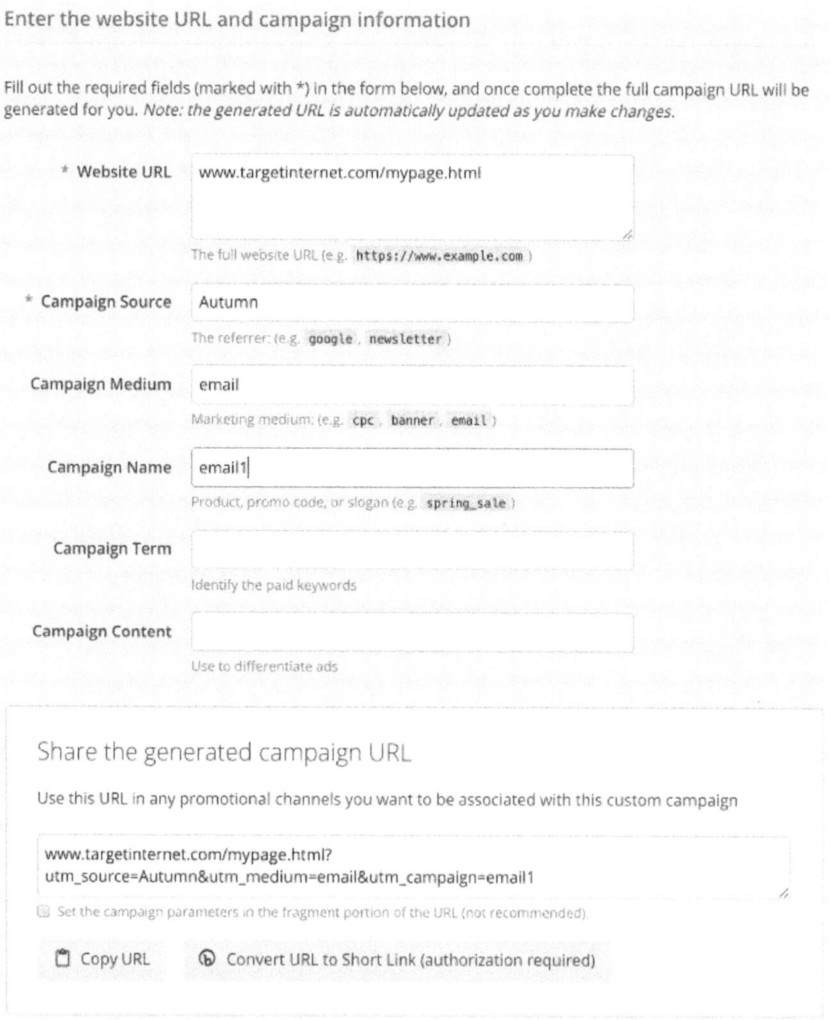

Enter the website URL and campaign information

Fill out the required fields (marked with *) in the form below, and once complete the full campaign URL will be generated for you. *Note: the generated URL is automatically updated as you make changes.*

* Website URL	www.targetinternet.com/mypage.html
	The full website URL (e.g. `https://www.example.com`)
* Campaign Source	Autumn
	The referrer: (e.g. `google` , `newsletter`)
Campaign Medium	email
	Marketing medium: (e.g. `cpc` , `banner` , `email`)
Campaign Name	email1
	Product, promo code, or slogan (e.g. `spring_sale`)
Campaign Term	
	Identify the paid keywords
Campaign Content	
	Use to differentiate ads

Share the generated campaign URL

Use this URL in any promotional channels you want to be associated with this custom campaign

www.targetinternet.com/mypage.html?
utm_source=Autumn&utm_medium=email&utm_campaign=email1

Set the campaign parameters in the fragment portion of the URL (not recommended).

🗍 Copy URL   ⓑ Convert URL to Short Link (authorization required)

Selecting an email service provider

To really get the most out of email marketing we have said we need to focus on relevance. In order to do that we are going to need to think about segmenting our data, targeting the content, testing different elements of our campaigns and really making best use of the channel. In order to do that, and to make it easy to do, we need to select the right tool, and generally that will be some form of ESP. These tools generally work around three key areas: building, segmenting and targeting your email list, building and sending your emails, and finally giving you reporting on the results. Each of these areas can be extended to offer all sorts of functionality like scheduling, automatic triggering and social media integration, all of which we'll explore more later.

The key thing is, you don't want to get stuck with a system that limits your capability but you also don't want to pay for things that you don't need. We've highlighted Mailchimp as an example ESP here, but there are new entrants all the time and many are very similar. To help you choose, we've highlighted some of the key considerations below.

Enter the monkey

Mailchimp is a very popular and low-cost ESP. It has an intuitive interface, loads of advanced functionality and is one of the cheapest ESPs in the market. It is also fully geared up to help you build mobile-optimized campaigns. They charge by the size of your list rather than by how many emails you send, which can be a real cost saver if you are sending a lot of emails.

So what are the downsides? First of all, all support is done online, meaning you don't have an account manager you can call on. Also, it's a self-service system, and although the interface is very straightforward, it's down to you (although there is nothing stopping you from bringing in a third party to assist you). You also need to pay using a credit/debit card, meaning if you can't pay this way, it's not for you. Finally, if you need some form of customization or really advanced integration it may not be the right choice (although they do have an API that lets developers do all sorts of things with the system).

We love Mailchimp. We use it for our podcast and love the fact it means we can test and learn quickly and easily. There are lots of other ESPs out there, but Mailchimp is often a very good starting point and works really well for podcasters: http://www.mailchimp.com

Gaining opt-ins and building a list

In order to do any email marketing we are going to need to collect an email list, and the rules on how we can collect data change from country to country. The recent EU General Data Protection Regulation (GDPR) has tightened up the rules across Europe, and the key point from an email point of view is that you really need an active opt-in, and you need to be very clear in telling people what you are going to do with their data.

GDPR

If you are at all unsure about GDPR, it's really worth doing your homework and making sure you're clear on how it impacts you and what you need to do. Luckily there are a number of great guides out there, and the Litmus blog has a lot of very clear and useful content on the topic: https://litmus.com/blog/5-things-you-must-know-about-email-consent-under-gdpr

---

It's also not just a matter of following the rules, but really about following best practice in order to assure the quality of our lists and avoid annoying our target audience. Like many things in digital marketing, we tend to get distracted by volume when carrying out email campaigns, and the questions often asked after each campaign are, 'How many emails have we sent?' and 'How many people are on our lists?' What we should really be focusing on is the quality of our lists and the actual results our campaigns get. We actively don't want people on our list that don't want our emails, otherwise we are just creating a negative touchpoint that will damage our brand image. I'm sure you can think of at least one company that keeps emailing you with irrelevant or overly sales-based content, and over time it creates a negative impression of that brand.

Podcast sign-up forms

Rather than trying to collect huge amounts of data at the point of sign-up, which will be a barrier to getting opt-ins, I generally recommend you keep the amount of information you initially ask for to a minimum. You then have the opportunity to prove the value of your emails and then ask for more information by using surveys, questionnaires or polls on an ongoing basis. You also need to consider the types of data you may want to collect;

will you really use that data and is your ESP capable of storing it and using it? We may also want to think about how we are going to move this data between our ESP and our CRM system, so it's worth making sure these two systems can be integrated.

Mobile and sign-up forms

One of the greatest ongoing frustrations for mobile users is pop-over email sign-up forms. For example, you visit a website and are reading a great blog post. After a few seconds a pop-over form covers the page and asks you to sign up to the website's email list. This is no problem on a laptop; you simply click the close window button on the top right corner of the pop-over. Unfortunately, many of these pop-overs are not built with mobile users in mind, and the close button is unreachable on a mobile device, leaving the user stranded on a useless page. If you are going to use pop-over forms, it is essential to thoroughly test them on mobile devices.

The two key things that concern people when they are signing up to an email list are what you are going to do with their data and how often you are going to email them. Ideally at this stage you will clarify both points with a statement along the lines of, 'We will never pass on your details to anybody else and we won't email you more than once a week'. You can also have a link through to your privacy policy that outlines clearly what you do with data, but in my experience very few people actually read these.

List segmentation

As you build an email list, you need to consider what differentiates the individuals on your list and what kinds of different content may be relevant to each of these segments. It's essential that your ESP allows you to collect data and add fields of information to your list in a way that will be practically useful for segmenting your lists in the future.

For example, you may want to send different emails to people living in different geographical locations or with different core interests and you'll therefore need to collect and store that data. Different ESPs have different approaches and limitations to this, but increasingly many ESPs allow you add a huge number of additional fields (in some cases an unlimited amount) that you can then use to segment and personalize your email.

***

The benefits and risks of personalization

Personalization in emails generally often refers to the process of inserting personalized content such as an individual's name, job role, company name or location into an email. It can also refer to the process of segmentation or dynamically building content, but we'll explore these concepts later.

So if we are talking about inserting a name into an email to personalize it, what actual impact does that have? Different studies show different results, and it certainly has to be seen in the context of your overall email efforts, but there is generally a small increase in CTR. However, if you get the data wrong and insert the wrong job title or name, the damage will far outweigh any good you would have done. Therefore, only do this form of personalization if you trust the quality of your data 100 per cent.

***

We can segment our lists in a number of different ways but we are generally talking about doing it based on collected data and by preference. This basically means that we have collected some information from an individual on our list and then use this to personalize their email. This may be in the form of sending particular content, sending a particular format of email or sending at a particular time or frequency, all based on the data you have collected.

Open rates and click-through rates

Two of the most commonly discussed statistics we get from our email campaigns are open rates and click-through rates. It's worth looking at these in a bit more detail so we understand where they are useful and what their limitations are.

Open rate tries to tell you how many people have actually opened your email. I say tried, because unfortunately, due to the way it is calculated it is inherently inaccurate. An email is registered as open when an image in that email has been loaded. So, you bring an email up in your email client, one of the images loads and that tells the ESP that the email must have been opened. This image is generally a single-pixel image hidden at the bottom of your email, often referred to as a web beacon. There are two problems with this approach. The first is that even if you open an email for half a second and then delete it, as long as the image loads, the email will show as having been opened. Now although this is technically true, the open rate doesn't really

paint a true picture of what happened for us. The other problem with relying on images being loaded to indicate an email being opened is that when
an email is viewed on an email client that doesn't load the images, you won't
know it has been opened. It has been suggested that around 50 per cent of
users don't see images automatically, which could mean some fairly unreli-
able data being reported as open rates.

However, this doesn't mean we should abandon looking at open rates. In
fact, we are still using them as a benchmark as at least we are comparing like
for like from one campaign to the next or within split testing (which we'll
talk about more in a moment). We just can't rely on them as an entirely accurate representation of how many people open our emails.

Click-through rate (CTR) is the other key measure we tend to look at,
and although it is far more accurate, we can rely on it too much. Obviously,
getting a click on your email and driving a visit through to your website is
great, but that is just part of the journey. It is entirely possible that everybody that clicks gets through to your website, takes one look, doesn't like
the look of it and leaves immediately. You could therefore have a campaign
with a 100 per cent CTR that is a complete failure!

So CTR is a useful measure but we then need to look at the visitor behaviour on our site to really understand the true impact of our email campaigns.
So for true commercial insights we will need email reporting, web analytics
and for goals to be set up in analytics. We'll also need to understand how
these goals impact our business outcomes (and that's what the final section
of this book is all about).

This does highlight one of the potential weaknesses of email marketing,
however, and that is that even if you have the best email campaigns in the
world, if your website doesn't match that standard, your campaign won't be
as effective as it could be.

Email templates and design

We could fill an entire book with the discussions about email design best
practice, what works and what doesn't. The reason for this level of discussion is that how effective the design is will depend on your target audience,
the email client and device the email is being read on and a host of other
factors. What that means is that we need to test for our particular list, and
in fact we may find that different designs are more or less suitable for different lists and even segments of our lists. We'll explore all the different things

you can test for your particular list later in this chapter, but we'll highlight here the key principles that every email should take into account.

Minimum font size

Apple recommends 17–22 pixels (px) and Google recommends 18–22px for mobile devices, so go for 18px minimum.

Header images above the fold

Don't place large header images at the top of emails. They push your content further down the page, and when images are switched off your audience won't see anything apart from a missing image.

Blocked images display

Consider what your email will look like when images are switched off. Make sure you have a 'click to view online' link (most ESPs will add these automatically). Also, make sure all of your images have ALT text as this will display in place of the image in many email clients when images are switched off.

Call to action placement and size

Consider where on the page your call to action will appear in various email clients and try and keep it visible above the fold (before a user needs to scroll down to see the content). Bear in might the bottom right, where many calls to action end up, may not be the most suitable place and you may need multiple calls to action.

For call to action buttons, Apple recommends 44px squared and Google recommends 48px squared for mobile users, so go for the higher of the two, 48px.

Scanability

Users try to assess the relevance of an email as soon as they open it and decide if it is worth reading properly or not. Make sure your email is scanable and that the key message comes across clearly and easily. Avoid large blocks of text, complicated layouts and poorly defined calls to action. Don't have multiple links close together.

Unsubscribe

Every email should have an unsubscribe link in the footer and this will generally be automatically inserted by your ESP.

Footer

The footer of your email should also include your physical postal address if you wish to be compliant with US email regulations (CAN-SPAM Act 2003).

Email templates

You have a few options to consider when creating emails and the templates that you use. You can design your own templates from scratch, edit an existing template from your ESP or use a template from another source. Each of your emails could be different, but in terms of brand consistency it makes sense to modify a particular template for a particular style of email each time you send one. So for example you may have a newsletter template, a commerce template, etc.

Most ESPs will provide a set of standard email templates that you can modify for your own use and many also provide a visual editor that lets you edit these templates without any coding skills. Alternatively you may need to edit your template code yourself and upload the HTML. You could do this editing yourself if you have the skills or use a designer/developer to do it for you. There are a lot of ESPs that offer these kinds of services at an additional cost or you could use a freelancer website like Upwork.com. Always remember, though, that email template design is a very specific skill, and just because somebody can design a website, it doesn't mean they know all the peculiarities of design for the wide range of email clients.

The most important thing to do with your email template is to make sure it displays properly on different email clients and devices, and to do this you have two options: one easy and one hard! The hard option is to manually test your email template on every possible different email client and device combination. This very quickly becomes an impractical task because of the number of possible options. This is why inbox inspectors were created, in order to simulate what your email will look like on each of these different display possibilities. Many ESPs have these built in, but if your system doesn't you can use a system like Litmus.com.

Spam checking

We've already discussed the improvements in technology that are leading to increased detection of spam emails. Unfortunately the side effect of this is that your email could be mistaken for spam by the many spam filters in operation and never reach its intended destination. In order to minimize the chances of this happening you can use a spam filter testing tool. This will try to gauge the likelihood of your email ending up in a spam filter and will point out any key things you may want to change.

Your ESP should have one of these tools built in, but if it doesn't, Litmus. com also offers this service.

Sending and testing

Once you have created your great email content and built the perfect targeted list, you're going to want to start sending your emails. There are quite a few things to consider at this stage and a range of testing options are available to you.

Many ESPs will now allow you to carry out A/B split testing very easily, or you can manually split up your list in order to do this. The basic principle is that you take two segments of your lists and send each a variation of your email, testing a particular feature of the email (this could be subject line, copy length, etc and we highlight these different variables in a moment). You then learn from these tests, work out which one got the best results and apply this learning to the remainder of your list. For example, you could take two segments of your list, each consisting of 15 per cent of the total list, and run a test (making up 30 per cent of your list overall). You then learn from this list and send out the better variation to the remaining 70 per cent of your list.

Open rate or click-through rate

When carrying out these tests, depending on what element of our email we are testing, we will need to look to the open rate or the CTR for our results to judge which is the most successful. We can split which of these two measures we need to look at as follows:

Open rate: subject line, time sent, from address.

CTR: all variations within the email content.

Once we decide which element of our email we are going to test, we also need to decide how long we are going to wait after sending the initial two tests until we judge the most successful and send it to the rest of our list.

Something you do need to consider, however, is the impact of the period of time you wait after sending your initial emails before you send to the remainder of your lists. If you send out the test segments on a Tuesday and then send out to the remainder of your list on a Wednesday, you will potentially skew your results, because people react differently to emails on different days of the week.

You could wait a clear seven days and send your follow-up email at the same time of day and day of the week as your test email, but even then you may find that things have changed over a week due to the time-sensitive nature of your news story or similar.

There is actually no 100 per cent ideal solution to this problem, but what you should do is understand which days of the week work best for you and how different days of the week compare. You can then choose to send your test and follow-up emails on days of the week when your audience reacts in similar ways.

Dynamic content generation and rules

So far we have talked about building a list, potentially segmenting this list up and then sending out content, with various testing opportunities. Many ESPs allow you to take your email marketing a stage further and generate even more segmented and personalized emails. They do this by not only looking at preference data – data that has been collected from the individual – but by also collecting behavioural data, dynamically generating emails based on this.

This could be as simple as triggering an email a month since the last email click-through. It could, however, be a lot more complex, looking at behaviour on your website and using this in order to adjust what content is sent out in an email. If an individual looks at a particular product, why not send them an email about that product? If they put an item in their basket and didn't buy it, why not send a follow-up email? Why not customize the content in the next email based on what they have clicked on in the last five emails? Different ESPs allow you to do different things, so it's worth considering from the outset the kind of dynamic personalization you may want to carry out. Some ESPs take this even further by thoroughly integrating with CRM systems and we could even then start to look at the topic of marketing automation. Tools like Salesforce and ActiveCampaign offer the functionality of ESP, CRM and marketing automation all in one system.

Email marketing conclusions

Email marketing is a hugely flexible area that can play an extremely effective part in your podcasting marketing. It is also something that can be done badly very easily, so a suitable level of planning and resourcing is essential to get it right. Selecting the right ESP will impact everything you do in your email marketing efforts, so select carefully and then make sure you are making full use of the various targeting and testing opportunities.

4 Paid search

We looked at search engine optimization along with the importance of landing pages for podcasting in Chapter 12. Pay per click (PPC) is the other side of search. We'll look at the pros and cons of PPC in detail, but its key advantage is our ability to control and target it precisely.

So how does paid search fit in with podcasting? It is not about display; that is, it's not about your ad showing up and having an impact on your branding by being seen, even though people don't click on it. This is about direct response and driving your audience through to your podcast landing pages at an appropriate stage in the user journey.

If you receive a promise of number one rankings in search from an agency or freelancer, one of two things is happening. They are either talking about PPC, or they are lying. No one can guarantee you number one rankings on Google, even someone who has done it a thousand times before, because only Google controls it.

Using PPC to build a podcast audience is not a particularly common tactic, but because of that, it's not particularly competitive and therefore, as you'll see, it's not always very expensive. If I search for a 'digital marketing podcast' and I'm not showing up in the organic search, a PPC ad will potentially get a click from someone who is actively interested in the topic.

Another major advantage of PPC is speed. You can be number one in the search rankings almost immediately if you are willing to pay for it. It can take months to achieve rankings for competitive terms with organic search, and even then it is not guaranteed. Also, don't mistake organic search for being free. Although you don't pay for every click, you will spend time and effort creating content and so on.

PPC is an auction-based system. The more you are willing to pay per click, the more visibility your ad will generally get. This also means that the more competitive your particular industry is, and the words that you choose to target, the more expensive it can become.

PPC fundamentals

The key steps involved in planning and implementing a successful mobile PPC campaign are:

- keyword research;
- create ad copy;
- select additional ad features;
- set targeting criteria;
- set budgets and bids.

PPC keyword research

There will certainly be commonality between this and the keyword research you do for your SEO campaigns, and you will use the same tools. However, one fundamental to understand about PPC is that the more precise your selection of words, and the better matched these are to your ad copy and landing pages, the more successful your campaign will be.

The words you select for your PPC campaigns will trigger your ads. You could select a generic search term to trigger your ad so that you get lots of traffic, but this is a very good way to spend lots of money and get few results. You could also use lots of different search terms to trigger the same generic ad; again, a good way to waste your budget. Generally, a very specific key phrase that triggers a specific ad, and which sends the searcher to a very specific and relevant landing page, will get the most from your budget.

Create ad copy

Fundamentally, a PPC ad is made up of a number of lines of text and a link through to your site (or a number of links). This copy is what grabs the searcher's attention and attracts the click-through to your site. We won't go into copywriting techniques here, as much has been written on the topic already, but the wording of your ads need to reflect the right context.

Bear in mind that you can create multiple versions of your ad copy and most PPC systems will automatically rotate these ads and tell you which one is attracting the most clicks and/or conversions on your site.

Additional ad features

Google (and Baidu) offers a number of additional ad options to enhance your PPC ads. An example in Google is that you can include links to multiple pages of your website. You can also add to your ads links to maps of your location.

These additional ad features serve two purposes. First, they clearly encourage users to take an action in response to your ads. Second, they can make it more likely your ad will be noticed in the first place as they differentiate it visually and generally add to its overall size.

Set targeting criteria

You can target by location-based criteria, which is split into three key areas in Google (most other systems follow similar principles, although accuracy can be poor in Baidu in particular):

- targeting by the physical location where the search is made (eg searching for 'hotels' while in New York);
- targeting by what people are searching for (eg searching for 'hotels in New York');
- targeting by intent – this is based on various factors that Google consider, such as previous searches (eg searching for 'hotels' after having searched 'trip to New York' and 'best deals flights New York').

Set budgets and bids

As well as setting your daily budget (the maximum you are willing to spend each day) you can set your maximum cost per click (CPC). CPC is the main factor that decides where your ad shows up on the page. Because PPC systems generally work on an auction basis, the more you are willing to pay per click, the higher up the page your ad appears and the more visibility it has. That visibility should lead to clicks, assuming your ad content is appealing to the searcher. You should not always assume, however, that it is always better to be in the top positions on the page. You may find that being further down the page means you are paying less per click and getting clicks more slowly, but you get better value overall from your budget. This is one of the many reasons that in order to get the maximum value from your budget you need to test and adjust your campaigns on an ongoing basis.

CPC can be set at a number of different levels. You can apply a single maximum CPC to a group of ads or just for a particular key phrase. Many systems, including Google, have an automatic bidding option that will try to maximize the number of clicks you receive for your budget. Just remember, though, that the maximum volume of traffic does not necessarily mean the maximum amount of conversions on your site.

Within Google Bid Adjustments, you can also adjust your bids according to contextual information such as mobile devices and time of day. For example, you may decide that mobile searches are more likely to convert into business, so you may be willing to pay more for a mobile click.

Within Google Ads you also have the option to set rules-based bidding, meaning that you do things like automatically adjust your bid (within a certain range) to always keep your ad in a certain position. This can help you to automate your bidding in order to factor in changes in competition levels.

PPC considerations

Beyond the fundamentals of PPC, there are some other things we need to consider when planning our campaigns that can have a significant impact on what value we get for our budgets.

Ongoing management and optimization

To get the most out of your PPC budgets your campaigns will need to be closely monitored, tested and adjusted on an ongoing basis. Levels of competition can change, and bids will need to change accordingly. You may find that certain keywords are working well and that others, although driving traffic, are not converting into business. Again, you will need to adjust your campaigns accordingly. This means that as well as considering the cost of your PPC budgets you need to factor in the time or cost of managing your campaigns effectively.

Quality scoring and Ad Rank

The Google Adwords system is particularly focused on rewarding campaigns that are highly targeted and give relevant results to searchers. It does this by factoring in a quality score when deciding what ads to show and how high up the page those ads should be displayed. Quality score takes into account a number of factors but looks at things like the click-through rate (CTR) of your ad in order to signify its relevance. This means that ads that are seen as being relevant are given a boost in their positioning and you can actually have your ad appearing above that of someone else who is actually paying more per click than you.

Other quality factors include having the word/phrase that was searched for actually in your ad and on the landing page that you are sending searchers through to.

Your quality score is combined with other factors, such as how much you are bidding and the expected impact of the ad format you use, to give you an overall 'Ad Rank'. This Ad Rank decides where your ad shows up.

The more relevant your ad, the better your quality score and the more visibility you get for your budget. It also means that Google is rewarding relevant ads, which in turn means that searchers see PPC ads as more relevant generally, and thus should in turn click on the ads more, thus making Google more money. Clever stuff.

SEO and PPC working together

We need to consider how SEO and PPC can work together effectively as part of our digital branding. I'm often asked whether you should bother with PPC advertising if you are already ranking number one for a search term in the organic search results. The only way to truly get an answer to that question is by testing it. Look at your results with and without PPC running and you answer the question precisely. This testing is even more necessary with mobile search, because of the different user focus and motivations. You will certainly get some cannibalization – people clicking on your paid ads who would have clicked on your organic search results – but you need to understand what additional traffic you can get and then look at how PPC and SEO traffic convert differently.

Paid search conclusions

Search is an effective and essential part of your podcast marketing toolkit and will make up an essential part of the user journey. Making sure we fully understand our target audience, their motivations and requirements, and mapping this to the content we provide (and optimize), is a fundamental requirement for any podcast to be really successful.

References and further reading

Facebook trust

Weisbaum, H (2018) Trust in Facebook has dropped by 66 percent since the Cambridge Analytica scandal, *NBC* [online] https://www.nbcnews.com/business/consumer/trust-facebook-has-dropped-51-percent-cambridge-analytica-scandal-n867011

Email response rates

MacDonald, S (2019) The science behind email open rates (and how to get more people to read your emails), *Superoffice* [online] https://www.superoffice.com/blog/email-open-rates/

The value of web analytics 24

Measuring the impact of your podcast activity

In this chapter, we will walk you through the enormous potential of web analytics and how you can use it to measure the impact of your podcasting. Most organizations now have web analytics (unlike five years ago) so there is usually now plenty of data available to assess campaigns. This data isn't always put to use in a productive way, though, and many organizations have more data than they know what to do with. There is much more to web analytics than simply producing a chart once a month to show an increase in web traffic. Many organizations need to learn to dig deeper and use the data available to them to explain why they are seeing certain trends and how things could be improved. The data is just the beginning; it's what you do with it that counts.

Making the most of Google Analytics

Google Analytics is an incredible tool. It's free and has over 86 per cent share of the global analytics market (W3Techs, 2018). Throughout this chapter, we're going to look at how you can use it to make the most of your podcasting, particularly within mobile sites and apps.

Before delving into the practicalities let's start with a brief introduction to Google Analytics. People often wonder why such a useful tool is available for free, considering that it provides hundreds of built-in reports and customization options, is reliably updated and offers the same as, if not more than, many commercial analytics packages. It did, in fact, start off as a commercial tool called Urchin but Google bought it, repackaged it and decided to give it away so that website owners could improve their sites and therefore their revenue. Why would Google care about this? Because their advertising products generate 86 per cent of their income (Rodriguez, 2018) and the more money you're earning through your website, the more likely you are to spend money on their advertising products.

It is possible to pay for a version of Google Analytics which offers even more than the free version. Google Analytics Premium gives enhanced functionality, customization and data access as well as things like an account manager, support over the telephone and a service level agreement. It is aimed at large organizations, so it is expensive (US $150,000 per year in fact). This isn't bad value though, considering what you get.

Getting started: setting up with Google Analytics

As with most analytics packages, Google Analytics uses something called 'page tagging' which allows them to gather information whenever someone uses your website pages or app screens (see the below box for more on apps). After registering for an account, Google Analytics will provide you with a unique code which you will need to put on every page of your website. This code then sends Google the information that they need. The data will include a range of mobile-specific reports.

What about apps?

Google Analytics can be used for apps as well as websites, although the process is slightly different. Once you have your account you'll to need to add a new 'property' (a property could be a website or an app). This app property will have a unique code which needs to be built into your app. You will likely need an app developer to do this for you as it is more complicated than simply adding it to every page of a website.

The main differences between app analytics reports and website analytics reports are that app reports will talk about screens rather than pages, and they will also report on 'events'. An event is something that occurs within a screen in your app without needing another screen to load. Web analytics reports do sometimes talk about events, but you are much more likely to come across them when thinking about mobile apps.

The key reports to be aware of

Once you've completed these initial steps and have your analytics codes, you will start to receive reports on visitors to your website or app. These reports will be broken down into the following key categories.

Real time

These reports give you information about people using your website or app in real time. You can do such things as track how people have found your website or app (for example via a link from another website or a search engine), you can see what they are looking at, or where they are located in the world. While it can be very interesting to track people in real time, these reports aren't, in fact, very useful. It can be utterly absorbing to see a real-time reaction to an email or social media campaign, but it's not actually that easy to do anything useful with the data. So beware – whilst this process might be fun, it will probably end up being a complete waste of your time!

Audience

As the name suggests, an audience report gives you information about the people using your website or app. It will tell you where they are in the world, or the technology that they are using, including the type of mobile device and operating system. Understanding what technology is being used to access your website or app is fundamentally important.

Acquisition

Acquisition reports used to be called 'traffic sources'. These reports can be used to see where your visitors are coming from and which of your digital channels are driving the most traffic to your website or app. Visitors to your site might have come from social media sites, search engines, other websites or they might be direct traffic. If traffic comes from another website this is called a referral. When we talk about direct traffic, we mean that users have simply typed your website address into their browser or clicked on a book-mark they have already saved. All this really means is that Google is unable to see where the traffic is coming from (we'll look at this in more detail later in reference to the tracking code). One thing to note at this point is that you can't visit a website by clicking on a podcast, so podcasts cannot drive traffic in this way. What they can do, however, is drive traffic from other channels such as search, or from social media, where your podcast content might be featured.

Using advanced segments to understand the user journey

Advanced segments is an incredibly useful feature of Google Analytics but it is often not used to its full potential. You can use it to view all of the key reports per segment of your audience, which is obviously really handy when trying to understand different user journeys and each touchpoint of your digital branding. You can either select single segments or multiple ones and analyse these on the same report. There are pre-determined segments or you can customize your own.

Behaviour

These reports were previously called 'content reports' and, unsurprisingly, they show you what users are up to on your site and allow you to see your most sought-after content. Using these reports, you'll be able to tell how long users are viewing certain pages, your bounce rates (ie how often someone enters your site and exits from the same page) and exit rates (ie the last page in someone's visit). These reports can come in very handy when trying to understand how people are using your podcast, for example, your show notes and other landing pages.

A note on bounces

Bounces are often thought of as a negative thing, but this is not necessarily true. Sure, it wouldn't be ideal for someone to enter your site and leave it 30 seconds later because they didn't like the look of it. This would be considered a bounce, and it is not what you want. However, a bounce could also come from someone who had bookmarked your blog so that they could read it regularly. They might land on your blog page, read it for half an hour and then leave, thereby entering and leaving your site via the same page. In the latter scenario the user got what they wanted, demonstrating that not all bounces should be viewed in the same way.

Conversions

When considering your digital branding, you cannot get a more important set of reports than the conversion reports. You might remember from earlier in the book that a conversion happens when someone completes one of your online goals, and as such they are closely associated with your business objectives.

You may also remember that a goal is something we hope a user will do on our site; for example, we might want them to buy something, fill in a lead-generation form, or click on an ad. A goal could be anything associated with your business objectives. Goals are not previously set up within standard analytics packages, so you will have to do this yourself within the admin functionality. Let's have a quick look at the different types of goals you might want to set up:

URL destination: we can often set this up as a 'thank you' page to thank the user for completing one of our goals, for example, downloading something ('thank you for downloading') or buying something ('thank you for buying'). Once a user gets to one of these pages, we know that they have carried out one of our goals.

Visit duration: if one of your goals is to build awareness, then understanding how long visitors are staying on your site could be helpful, as this would indicate that they are using and are interested in your content.

Pages per visit: you might want to set this up as a goal if you'd like visitors to view multiple pages on your site. Bear in mind, though, that somebody viewing lots of pages isn't necessarily a good thing, as it might just mean that they can't find what they're looking for!

Event: if somebody does something within a page of your website, this is known as an 'event'. It would therefore be helpful to set this up as a goal if you wanted users to, for example, fill in a form or download something. If you wanted to track events within a page, however, you would need to add extra code to the web pages.

Once you start to get goal reports, you can use them alongside your advanced segments reports to identify completed goals from particular traffic sources.

Using 'multichannel funnels' reporting

If you want to understand how your different marketing activities are affecting your conversion rates then multichannel funnels reporting is what you need. Goal reports do have their limitations and can be misleading because they go by the 'last click', meaning that they tell you the traffic source that sends a user to your site, without considering what might have gone on before. Consider the following example: a user performs a Google search and, as a result of the search, enters your website and downloads something. The search would be recorded as the source of the goal. However, this user might have received an email a week before and already visited your website, but without downloading anything. Once they return a week later, this time using Google to search for your website, the source of the conversion would be considered the search without recognizing the significant part played by the email.

This is where multichannel funnels reporting comes into its own. This extremely powerful and clever reporting system can record all of the different sources of traffic that contribute towards the conversion of your goals. These reports will be able to tell you if, for example, users are first visiting your site via referrals from social media sites and then returning at a later date via search and completing your goals. They even show the percentages that different traffic sources have contributed towards your conversions. Figure 24.1 shows how we can use multichannel funnels reporting to gain a much fuller picture of the user journey.

Additional learning material for analytics

There are a couple of really good learning resources you can use if you need a bit more guidance with these reports. They are both from Google and won't cost you anything.

Analytics Academy. These are online, interactive tutorials which give you a step-by-step guide to the key reports: https://analytics.google.com/analytics/academy/

Google Analytics YouTube channel. This is likely to answer just about any question you might have about Google Analytics. It includes Web Analytics TV and user questions are answered by Avinash Kaushik and Nick Mihailovski. We would highly recommend it: https://www.youtube.com/user/googleanalytics

Figure 24.1 'Multichannel funnels' reporting

Multichannel Conversion Visualizer

See the percentage of conversion paths that included combinations of the channels below. Select up to four channels.

Direct & Organic Search & Paid Search: 2.85% (174)

Channel	% of total conversions
Direct	78.62%
Organic Search	43.27%
Paid Search	6.69%
Referral	5.62%
Email	2.48%
Social Network	0.95%
Display	0.20%

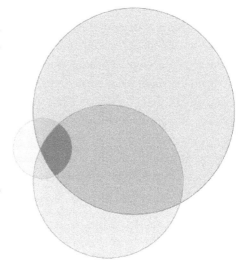

The overlap areas of the circles above are approximations

(Google and the Google logo are registered trademarks of Google Inc, used with permission.)

Adding in tracking code

We mentioned tracking code earlier in relation to the acquisition reports and direct traffic. Analytics tracking code may be necessary to track some sources of traffic through your site if Google cannot tell where it is coming from. If, for example, you decided to place different versions of an ad on the same website, adding tracking code to a weblink will help you to determine the traffic source. Let's use an example to consider this in a little more detail.

You decide to add a link in your email to drive traffic to your website, but you don't add tracking code. Without tracking code, Google cannot tell where clicks from an email have come from (unless it is webmail), and so will record the visit as direct traffic, which is not particularly useful if you're trying to understand your email visitors. Therefore, if we want to be able to fully analyse our email visitors and fully understand the impact of our email campaigns, we need to add tracking code to all of our links.

The good news is that Google provides us with a tool to generate tracking code and it is a very straightforward process:

- Step 1: Search 'Google URL builder' (an online form for generating the code).

- Step 2: Enter the page you want to link to and fill in the required fields on the form. This will generate a new link that includes the tracking code.

- Step 3: Add this link to your email. Now when a user clicks on it, Google Analytics will record it as 'campaign traffic'. It will also report any other details that you entered into the URL builder, such as the name you gave it.

This same process can be used for generating tracking code for ads, email and links in social media, and is crucial in order to gain a deeper understanding of which links are driving traffic to your site. This is particularly important if you are implementing digital marketing dashboards, so that you can understand the contribution of different social media sites, etc.

How web analytics can be used in relation to our podcasting activity

So how should we be using web analytics in relation to podcasting? Ideally, we would want it to demonstrate that our podcasting is helping to achieve our business objectives. We could do this by using a multichannel funnels report to help us track and analyse traffic generated by our podcasting activity. Things we would want to look out for include:

- an increasing amount of traffic to our podcast pages;
- an increasing amount of traffic to other content signposted in our podcasts;
- traffic from the digital channels used to signpost podcast content including pages linked to from email, social media, display and paid search campaigns associated with our podcasting, and podcast landing pages.

Web analytics could also help us to identify any patterns in search traffic for terms related to our podcast or topics discussed within it. It can be intriguing to compare any growth in our podcast listeners with any growth in direct traffic but it's not the most reliable of activities, as it's hard to prove a link between the two.

Analytics: key takeaways

Web analytics provides us with enormous amounts of potential for gaining a better understanding of our audience and their user journeys towards completing our goals. However, we need to spend some time getting to know the tools available to us and ensuring that we use them effectively in order to plan our podcasting marketing activities so that we can make meaningful links between our podcast users and our business objectives.

References and further reading

Google Analytics usage

W3Techs (2018) Usage statistics and market share of Google Analytics for websites [online] https://w3techs.com/technologies/details/ta-googleanalytics/all/all

Google revenue

Rodriguez, A (2018) It's not all about advertising at Alphabet anymore, *Quartz* [online] https://qz.com/1334369/alphabet-q2-2018-earnings-google-is-more-than-just-advertising-now/

Part Four
The future of podcasting

Where next for podcasting? 25

Conversational design, artificial intelligence and machine learning

There are a range of trends in digital marketing and technology being touted as potential game changers for podcasting. Topics like the increased use of messenger bots, artificial intelligence (AI) and the rise of personal assistant speakers in our homes have given rise to conversations about how podcasts could radically change. Podcast hosts could be AIs; we would be able to automatically create a podcast using a simulated voice and grabbing information from the web. Although these technologies will change podcasting, it won't be quite the radical change we've just suggested. Podcast production may get easier (more on that in a moment) but what makes podcasts great is also what prevents them from being changed too radically.

A quick note on messenger bots and conversational design

In case you're not familiar, messenger bots are those little chats that can be launched from a website or app, which give you automated assistance and conversation. These don't generally use AI (but they can) but rather just clever scripting and conversation options. This scripting is known as conversational design, and although many current messenger bots are disappointing, this is generally down to poor conversational design. For some great insights and examples take a look at the work of the very talented Henry Burton, whom we interview on the topic for our own podcast: https://www.artelligen.com/

Radio has been much the same, in terms of format and physical consumption, since its inception. We may have developments like digital radio, internet radio, high-compression streaming and crystal clear sound, but essentially we are still listening, via our human ears, to human voices, music and other sounds in the same way. That is because at the heart of these experiences is the human voice and narrative, and those are two things that have never changed, and won't in the foreseeable future. Yes, we can simulate the human voice more effectively, but the conversations we have and the nuances of human language are still a long way off from being equalled by an AI, and this is basically because they are so complex. We are certainly making great leaps in AI, but these kinds of achievements are a way off (although we also fully expect to read this chapter within our own lifetimes and for it to be completely wrong).

AI vs machine learning

The term 'artificial intelligence' can be a little misleading, with people thinking it's all about interacting with some sort of intelligent agent that can have a smart conversation with you. There are many types of AI, and increasingly the term 'machine learning' is being used instead. They are essentially referring to the same things but machine learning is probably better at setting an expectation of what we are actually getting. You actually have machine learning on your phone right now (if you have a reasonably modern smartphone). Go to your photo app, search for a particular thing, such as a dog, and it will be able to tell the difference between a human face and a dog face and return you a result if you have any pictures of dogs.

The Turing test

To put AI in perspective, let's take a look at the Turing test:

> The Turing test, developed by Alan Turing in 1950, is a test of a machine's
> ability to exhibit intelligent behaviour equivalent to, or indistinguishable from,
> that of a human. Turing proposed that a human evaluator would judge natural
> language conversations between a human and a machine designed to generate
> human-like responses. The evaluator would be aware that one of the two
> partners in conversation was a machine, and all participants would be separated
> from one another. The conversation would be limited to a text-only channel
> such as a computer keyboard and screen so the result would not depend on the

machine's ability to render words as speech. If the evaluator cannot reliably tell the machine from the human, the machine is said to have passed the test. The test results do not depend on the ability to give correct answers to questions, only how closely the answers resemble those a human would give.

This is the definition used on the Loebner Prize website, which is the oldest contest to see if anyone can pass the Turing test, and rewards anyone that does well with a series of prizes. No machine has ever passed the Turing test.

If we can't pass the Turing test, we're certainly not going to do it when we also have to create the nuances of the human voice. So where does this leave podcasting in regard to AI? Is it useless? No, it just isn't used in quite the way that people expect. At this point I'll hand you over to an expert on the topic, Jeremy Waite from IBM:

PODCAST INSIGHTS   Artificial intelligence and podcasts

Jeremy Waite, Chief Strategy Officer, IBM Watson Customer Engagement (and creator of the *10 Words* podcast)

How do I think it's going to be changing content creation in the future? What's the impact that AI is going to have? I'd point you towards two case studies. The first one is Wimbledon and the second one is Project Debater.

The thing is, AI can do a million different things and cover a multitude of sins: augmented intelligence, intelligent assistance and so on. They all do slightly different things. I work with Watson, which is an AI, but it's really just more of a toolbox of commands. It's based upon natural language processing and not all AIs are like that. So, Watson as an AI is understanding natural language, the tone, the sentiment and all the different types of speech analysis, voice to text, personality insights, what emotions are triggered by certain words and so on. So we've done this now with Wimbledon, where every single second of video footage for all the highlights is now 100 per cent done by Watson, with no human involvement whatsoever. Every piece of content is created by computer for Wimbledon live, within 10 minutes of the match ending, from scratch: https://www.ibm.com/thought-leadership/wimbledon/uk-en/

Project Debater is when you actually create a thought leadership piece based upon a point of view, where you've just fed a massive corpus of information into Watson, to create, on its own, an argument or a debate: https://www.research.ibm.com/artificial-intelligence/project-debater/

I think what it's going to do is help you with all the planning stage. So, my 15 hours might only take one hour to plan, but I think because of the lack of empathy that machines have, you're going to need real humans to put the actual content together themselves because humans connect with other humans. So this is where I always steal from Garry Kasparov, and say the best combination is a good human and a machine. It was a good 10 words to finish with!

Future-proofing your podcast strategy for the ever-changing user journey

We've already looked at a few of the emerging technologies and trends in digital, and what this might mean to our podcasting efforts. In an environment of constant change, particularly one as fast-paced as digital marketing, the only guarantee is that the pace of change will continue to grow, and this is the slowest it will be going forwards!

So how can we predict the future and make sure our podcasting efforts and the surrounding marketing we do are ready? We can't. But what we can do is go back to basics, and this will protect us from change long enough for us to adapt. So, what are the basics?

Content and narrative

As long as we focus on producing the highest quality of content we can, that is aligned with our target audience and their user journey, then we will be providing value. Providing value builds trust and loyalty.

Narrative is also key. We have been telling each other stories since the dawn of civilization, and these stories are what makes podcasting such a powerful medium. Whether you are trying to explain the latest digital marketing technology trend, or bringing to life a real-life crime drama, narrative is what makes it engaging and memorable.

We should never forget that podcasting is just telling stories.

Podcasting Toolkit

Throughout this book we've highlighted tools and techniques that you can try out and apply to your own podcasts. You'll find all of these compiled into the Podcasting Toolkit, as well as other resources (like the Podcasting Content Calendar) at: www.targetinternet.com/podcastbook

Thank you

We hope this book has inspired and encouraged you to create your own podcasts. We want to hear about what you've created and listen to your podcasts. You can get in contact via social media, email or our contact form, and you'll find all of our details here: www.targetinternet.com/contact

INDEX

Note: Page numbers in *italics* indicate figures or tables.

CPSIA information can be obtained
at www.ICGtesting.com
Printed in the USA
JSHW011653171121
20553JS00001B/26